COMPETITIVENESS OF THE U.S. MINERALS AND METALS INDUSTRY

Committee on
Competitiveness of the Minerals and Metals Industry

NATIONAL MATERIALS ADVISORY BOARD
COMMISSION ON ENGINEERING AND TECHNICAL SYSTEMS

NATIONAL RESEARCH COUNCIL

NATIONAL ACADEMY PRESS
Washington, D.C.
1990

NATIONAL ACADEMY PRESS • 2101 Constitution Avenue, N.W. • Washington, D.C.

This report was supported by the U.S. Department of the Interior, Bureau of Mines under Grant No. G0178055.

Library of Congress Cataloging-in-Publication Data

National Research Council (U.S.) Committee on Competitiveness of the
  U.S. Minerals and Metals Industry.
    Competitiveness of the U.S. minerals and metals industry : report
  of the Committee on Competitiveness of the U.S. Minerals and Metals
  Industry, National Materials Advisory Board, Commission on
  Engineering and Technical Systems, National Research Council.
      p. cm.
    Includes bibliographical references and index.
    ISBN 0-309-04245-3
    1. Mineral industries—United States. 2. Metal trade—United
  States. 3. Mineral industries. 4. Metal trade. 5. Competition,
  International. I. Title.
  HD9506.U62N34 1990
  338.2'0973—dc20   90-39804
                                                        CIP

Printed in the United States of America

NATIONAL ACADEMY OF ENGINEERING

2101 Constitution Avenue, N.W.
Washington, D.C. 20418

Office of the President

Mr. T S Ary
Director
Bureau of Mines
U.S. Department of the Interior
2401 E Street, N.W.
Washington, D.C. 20241

Dear Mr. Ary:

I am pleased to transmit a report on <u>The Competitiveness of the Minerals and Metals Industry</u>, prepared by the National Materials Advisory Board of the National Research Council (NRC). As with all reports of the NRC, the report is the responsibility of the committee, but its review has been monitored by the Academies' Report Review Committee.

The National Academy of Engineering (NAE) has long been concerned about the competitiveness of U.S. industry in an increasingly integrated global economy. The U.S. minerals industry was selected for study after an initial workshop in February 1986 that highlighted the increasing competitive pressures experienced by the industry. At the workshop it became apparent that a much larger effort would be required to assess the future health of the industry.

In June 1987, the Assistant Secretary for Water and Science of the Department of the Interior requested that we consider a study focused on the opportunities that would significantly improve the ability of U.S. producers to compete with foreign producers and the opportunities that exist for advanced materials and new technology to improve operating efficiency in the minerals industry. The issues raised by the Assistant Secretary were parallel to the concerns of the NAE and resulted in the present study funded by the Bureau of Mines.

The minerals industry contributes significantly to the nation's economic strength and represents a multi-billion dollar enterprise that employs on the order of one half million U.S. workers and provides much of the materials foundation for U.S. manufacturing. The report stresses that although the domestic industry is currently competitive, this competitiveness may be transitory. The competitiveness of the industry is based largely on non-technological measures that have already yielded many of their possible benefits. As a result, the domestic industry must in the future focus increasingly on other measures, most notably the use of technology.

The minerals and metals industry although unique in some respects is very much like most basic industries. It is noteworthy that the report echoes many of the recommendations of studies of other industries including the need for new mechanisms for conducting cooperative research and development between industry, universities, and the government.

It is our hope that the Bureau of Mines which has recognized the importance of maintaining the competitiveness in the U.S. minerals and metals industry will find the recommendations in this report useful in the formulation of policies and programs that can achieve this goal.

Sincerely,

Robert M. White
President

COMMITTEE ON COMPETITIVENESS OF
THE U.S. MINERALS AND METALS INDUSTRY

ALVIN W. TRIVELPIECE *(Chairman)*, Oak Ridge National Laboratory, Oak Ridge, Tennessee

ROBERT R. BEEBE *(Vice Chairman)*, Homestake Mining Company, San Francisco, California

GEORGE S. ANSELL, Colorado School of Mines, Golden

NATHANIEL ARBITER, Consultant, Vail, Arizona

PATRICK R. ATKINS, Aluminum Company of America, Pittsburgh, Pennsylvania

R. STEPHEN BERRY, University of Chicago, Chicago, Illinois

PETER CANNON, CONDUCTUS, Sunnyvale, California

JAMES ECONOMY, University of Illinois, Urbana

JAMES A. FORD, Consultant, Johnson City, Tennessee

NORMAN A. GJOSTEIN, Ford Motor Company, Dearborn, Michigan

BRUCE A. KENNEDY, P. T. Pelsart Management Services, Jakarta, Indonesia

WILLIAM W. LEWIS, McKinsey and Company, Washington, D.C.

JAMES S. MOOSE, The World Bank, Washington, D.C.

HAROLD W. PAXTON, Carnegie Mellon University, Pittsburgh, Pennsylvania

JOHN E. TILTON, Colorado School of Mines, Golden

A. DOUGLAS ZUNKEL, A. D. Zunkel Consultants, Inc., Vancouver, Washington

Liaison Representative

GEORGE WHITE, Bureau of Mines, Washington, D.C.

NMAB Staff

Lance N. Antrim, Project Officer
Robert M. Ehrenreich, Staff Officer
Courtland S. Lewis, Consultant/Writer
Paul B. Phelps, Editor
Mary W. Brittain, Administrative Officer
Aida C. Neel, Senior Secretary
Klaus M. Zwilsky, Staff Director

Abstract

This report of the Committee on Competitiveness of the Minerals and Metals Industry contains comprehensive assessments of the recent history and current structure of the global minerals and metals industry and of the competitive status of the U.S. industry within that global marketplace. The industry contributes significantly to the nation's economic strength and military security, representing a multibillion dollar enterprise that employed 500,000 U.S. workers in 1989 and provided the material foundation for U.S. manufacturing. The report assesses the technologies currently in use by the domestic industry and recommends research and development (R&D) needed to pursue future technologies. Projected trends in demand for metals are examined in light of increasing demand for and substitution by new materials. The nation's industrial and academic capabilities for R&D in these fields are evaluated, and human resource issues are discussed quantitatively. Federal support of mining- and metals-related R&D across all agencies is summarized. The federal role in support of this industry is discussed in depth, with a particular focus on the role of the Bureau of Mines. Minerals and metals policies of some other nations are briefly reviewed. Mechanisms for improving the development and implementation of new technologies by the domestic industry are suggested. Finally, a number of recommendations are directed at government, industry, and academe—recommendations that are intended to foster the development of partnerships among these three sectors for the pursuit of technology to improve the competitiveness of the U.S. industry.

Preface

Throughout the 1980s a dominant theme heard in Washington and in corporate boardrooms across the nation was concern about the declining competitiveness of U.S. industry. The decline of exports, jobs, and market share in one industry after another became almost a litany, as the nation's leaders struggled to understand the decline and find ways to reverse it. One of the hardest-hit industries was the minerals- and metals-producing industry, a diverse group of mining companies, mineral processors, and metal fabricators. The industry was facing intense competition not only from low-cost foreign producers of commodity minerals but also from alternative materials such as plastics, ceramics, and optical fibers. By late 1985, after four consecutive years of heavy losses, observers were predicting the "death of mining" in the United States and a very dim future for U.S. metals producers.

This prospect was of concern not only to the industry but also to many people in government, and in particular to the U.S. Department of the Interior and the Bureau of Mines. In June 1987 the Assistant Secretary of the Interior for Water and Science wrote to the president of the National Academy of Engineering (NAE) requesting a study of "the implications of materials science and engineering to the minerals producing industries." The NAE turned to the National Research Council (NRC), which initiated a study by the National Materials Advisory Board (NMAB) under the sponsorship of the Bureau of Mines.

Following discussions with Bureau of Mines representatives, NMAB developed a tentative set of objectives for the study. Essentially, the study would (1) seek to identify significant new technologies that might improve minerals production and processing, (2) attempt to gauge their likely impact on the competitiveness of the domestic industry, and (3) recommend ways to improve the development and implementation of technologies throughout the industry. The intent was to build on the parallel NRC study on Materials Science and Engineering for the 1990s and determine where and how science and technology could exert significant leverage to lower the cost or improve the performance of the products of the materials industry. An important underlying focus of both studies was on identifying ways in which the federal government can contribute to the effective application of technology in industry.

The Committee on Competitiveness of the Minerals and Metals Industry was formed by the NRC. The membership of the committee was selected to bring balanced and broad-based expertise to bear in addressing these issues.

As the committee was beginning its deliberations, however, conditions in the minerals and metals industry changed. In 1987 both prices and the demand for metals turned sharply upward. At the same time, the value of the dollar was declining against many major currencies, increasing demands for U.S. minerals. These trends generated a sudden and very welcome surge in profits for U.S. minerals and metals producers. Drastic restructuring undertaken over the preceding years had significantly reduced the size of the industry, but for the short term at least what remained of the industry was suddenly in an improved financial situation. Having seen numerous cycles of profit and loss in the past, however, committee members remained concerned about the long-term implications of this business revival. Nevertheless, the change in climate prompted the committee to take a step back from the immediate situation and address the longer-term technological basis of the industry and its interactions with its "support base" in government and academe. Thus, to the initial focus on specific technologies was added a second focus on long-range structural improvements to generate technology and put it into practice in the minerals and metals industry.

The committee organized itself into three working groups dealing with the structure of the industry, patterns of supply and demand, and the role of science and technology. The committee's efforts respectively became the basis for Chapters 1, 2, and 3. The committee as a whole participated in the formulation of institutional issues (Chapter 4), policy issues (Chapter 5), and of course in the recommendations (Chapter 6). The committee also held two workshops—"Changing Patterns of Supply and Demand" and the "Role of Science and Technology in the Competitiveness of the Minerals and Metals Industry"—and sought advice from many individuals in government, industry, and academe.

Perhaps the overriding conclusion of the committee is that, through cutbacks in funding for industry and academic research and development (R&D), through a loss of boldness in the R&D sponsored or performed by government laboratories, and through a lack of cooperation among the various sectors of the minerals and metals community, the "technology pipeline" for the domestic industry has all but dried up. Most of the committee's recommendations are intended to reopen that pipeline and stimulate a strong, steady flow of new technologies by fostering a three-way partnership between government, industry, and academe that will produce a coherent national program of mining and minerals R&D.

We believe that the committee's recommendations represent a roadmap for ensuring that the United States can continue to remain strong in providing competitive raw materials. This report is offered with the hope that its recommendations will be adopted by those who are responsible for decisions that will determine the future of the vital U.S. minerals and metals industry.

ALVIN W. TRIVELPIECE, *Chairman*
ROBERT R. BEEBE, *Vice Chairman*

Committee on Competitiveness of the
U.S. Minerals and Metals Industry

Acknowledgments

This study on the competitiveness of the diverse minerals and metals industry could not have been accomplished without the contributions of many individuals. The work of the committee was supported by the Bureau of Mines of the U.S. Department of the Interior, and we acknowledge this support with thanks. T S Ary, Director of the Bureau of Mines, maintained an active interest in the committee throughout the study. David S. Brown, Associate Director for Information and Analysis, and his deputy, Hermann Enzer, provided invaluable information to the committee. David R. Forshey, Associate Director for Research, and John Breslin, Chief of Staff for Research, supplied background and pertinent information requested by the committee. The chief of the Office of Mineral Institutes, Ronald Munson, also provided valuable information, as did Steven Hill, director of the Salt Lake City Research Center, and Lewis Wade, director of the Twin Cities Research Center. The Bureau of Mines Chief Staff Officer, John D. Morgan, provided valuable information related to policy from the minerals and metals standpoint. Additional information was supplied by James Donahue, chief of the Budget Office; William Schmidt and Philip Meikle, research program managers; and by many commodities specialists at the Bureau.

Presentations to the committee by experts from industry, academe, and government provided information that was instrumental in establishing the framework for the study. They are Paul H. O'Neill, Aluminum Company of America; John Alic, Office of Technology Assessment; Dodd A. Carr, International Lead-Zinc Research Organization; William Dennis, American

Iron & Steel Institute; William Drescher, International Copper Association; Douglas W. Fuerstenau, University of California at Berkeley; Carl Peterson, Massachusetts Institute of Technology; Bruce Tippen, University of Alabama; Dick J. Wilkins, University of Delaware; John C. Williams, U.S. Department of Commerce; William R. D. Wilson, Northwestern University; Jenifer Robison, Office of Technology Assessment; Hans Landsberg, Resources for the Future; William A. Owczarski, Office of Science and Technology Policy; David Bussard, U.S. Environmental Protection Agency; Simon D. Strauss, consultant; and Paul C. Maxwell, Committee on Science, Space, and Technology, U.S. House of Representatives.

The committee is also grateful for the information provided on academic programs, enrollments, and faculty members in the relevant fields by Eileen Ashford from the South Dakota School of Mines and Technology.

In addition, the committee appreciates the assistance of the many individuals in government agencies, including the National Science Foundation; U.S. Geological Survey; U.S. Department of Energy; National Institute of Standards and Technology; Defense Advanced Research Projects Agency, U.S. Department of Defense; National Oceanic and Atmospheric Administration; and the Minerals Management Service of the U.S. Department of the Interior. The committee also wishes to thank John A. White and John Larsen-Basse of the National Science Foundation for their assistance and for the information they provided.

Several industry associations are thanked for their help. They are the American Iron and Steel Institute, International Lead-Zinc Research Organization, International Copper Association, Nonferrous Metals Producers Group, American Mining Congress, Mining and Metallurgical Society of America, and the Mining and Excavation Research Institute.

The committee acknowledges and thanks the participants of the two workshops. The workshop on "Changing Patterns of Supply and Demand" was attended by R. O. Muth, ASARCO, and John K. Hammes, Citibank, and the workshop on the "Role of Science and Technology in the Competitiveness of the Minerals and Metals Industry" was attended by Roshan Bhappu, Mountain States Research and Development; David Bollin, Pincock, Allen, and Holt; Maurice A. Cocquerell, Acres Davy McKee Engineering; Maurice Davidson, Newmont Exploration; Terry P. McNulty, Hazen Research, Inc.; Ronald A.. Miller, Aluminum Company of America; Hayden Murray, Indiana University; M. D. Salamon, Colorado School of Mines; and Donald Steeples, Kansas Geological Survey.

The committee also wishes to acknowledge discussions with the several executives of mining companies who gave their candid assessments of the structure of the industry and their views on the future of research and development in the mining industry.

The committee is especially grateful for the assistance of George White,

Director of Special Projects, Bureau of Mines, who served as liaison to the committee. He obtained a great deal of information for the committee both in terms of Bureau reports and legislation and in presentations related to the structure, mission, and program of the Bureau.

Finally, we extend our appreciation to the staff of the National Materials Advisory Board for their support. They are Lance N. Antrim, project officer; Robert M. Ehrenreich, staff officer; Courtland S. Lewis, consultant/writer; Paul B. Phelps, editor; Mary W. Brittain, administrative officer; Aida C. Neel, senior secretary; and Klaus M. Zwilsky, director.

Contents

COMPETITIVENESS
OF THE
U.S. MINERALS
AND METALS INDUSTRY

Frontispiece: California hand jig, c. 1860; California placer gold gravity rocker, c. 1860 (Courtesy N. Arbiter); Gold operations: Round Mountain, NV and McLaughlin, Lower Lake, CA (Courtesy Homestake Mining Co., photographer Mickey Brim)

Executive Summary

The United States has consistently maintained that a strong domestic minerals and metals industry is an essential contributor to the nation's economic and security interests. Despite competition from foreign firms, the domestic industry has the potential to remain strong, but this potential cannot be realized without active support for the technological base of the industry. This base is threatened by the failure of industry, academe, and government to maintain the partnership that has contributed to a U.S. comparative advantage in technology for much of this century. A strategy of applying a technology-based comparative advantage can contribute to the competitiveness of the domestic industry, but its success requires rebuilding of the industry-academe-government partnership. All three groups must support the partnership, and the Bureau of Mines, as the responsible federal agency, must take an active role in maintaining it.

The United States has a fundamental interest in maintaining a competitive minerals and metals sector that will continue to contribute significantly to the nation's economic strength and military security. The industry represents an $87 billion enterprise that employs over 500,000 U.S. workers and provides the material foundation for U.S. manufacturing. Although the intensity of use of metals (i.e., per unit of gross national product) is expected to decline gradually over time, the long-term outlook is that continued growth of the economy will ensure increasing markets for metals. Metals in general continue to be very competitive with respect to alternative materials. Penetration of nonmetallics into traditional markets for metals will be slow and will take place largely on a part-for-part basis that limits the exploitation of the potential benefits of nonmetallics in competition with metals currently in use.

The United States is among the world's largest consumers of nearly every metal, much of which is imported. In 1988 the nation had a net trade deficit of $22.3 billion in nonfuel minerals and metals. Since many of the world's mineral resources are located in areas where political instability and/or economic manipulation represent a potential threat to supply, it is essential for the United States to ensure some degree of independence from foreign control over supply and costs through domestic participation in this industry. Congress, through successive legislative acts, has established a national policy to encourage a strong domestic industry. It specifically noted the importance of encouraging mining, mineral, and metallurgical research as part of this policy. The research and development (R&D) supporting the technology base for the industry has been a cooperative responsibility of industry, academe, and government.

The U.S. share of the world market for most major metals has slipped steadily over the past two decades; however, the domestic minerals and metals industry continues to compete on an international basis. The United States is among the world's largest producers of many important metals and still has substantial domestic reserves. One of the primary competitive advantages the United States enjoys over its strongest industrial competitors, Japan and Western Europe, is its domestic resource base. The domestic metals industry supplies about 50 percent of the metal used by the U.S. manufacturing industry, and the degree of competitiveness (defined in terms of market share, profitability, capacity utilization, and/or growth) varies across the particular metals subindustries.

The industry reached its present level of profitability after a protracted period of recession. The recession was accompanied by heavy financial losses, restructuring, rationalization, and capacity reduction. Factors that led to the turnaround included commodity price increases, favorable currency exchange rates, and reduced labor costs along with new applications of technology.

Unless a strategy building on areas of U.S. comparative advantage is pursued, the current competitiveness of the domestic industry versus foreign competitors is likely to be transitory. Nontechnological measures (such as plant closings, reduction of the labor force, and wage concessions) have already yielded most of their possible benefits. The potential for future gains in profitability from such adjustments is now much lower. As a result, the competitiveness of the domestic industry must in the future depend increasingly on other ir as i es, most notably technology. The pervading message of this report is the need to improve the technology base of the U.S. minerals and metals industry by increasing the amount and quality of research and development, as well as the speed with which the results are transferred to industrial applications.

TECHNOLOGY AND COMPETITIVENESS

A technology-based strategy can improve the long-term competitiveness of the minerals and metals industry. Technology can contribute to competitiveness by increasing productivity or product quality, by addressing circumstances unique to a process, company or country, or by assisting producers to adapt to changing consumer demand. A technology-based competitiveness strategy requires a continuing commitment to the development and application of technology. While the United States does not lag behind other nations in the relevant science and technology, the research has been insufficiently imaginative and communication between academic researchers and the engineers who deal with industrial problems has been poor.

Industry

While technology was not the only factor and would not have been sufficient alone, its importance was demonstrated in the recent recovery of the industry, in which new applications of technology played a very important role even though the technology used was for the most part off the shelf, a result of past R&D in the United States and abroad.

Although technologies can diffuse rapidly across international and corporate boundaries, it is still possible to create a comparative advantage from investments in R&D. One advantage comes from being the first to apply a technological advance, since a 2- to 3-year lead time usually accrues to the originator and first implementor of the technology. The rapid diffusion of the technology reduces but does not eliminate this advantage. Another advantage comes when the technology is related to special conditions not prevalent elsewhere (e.g., high labor costs, unique ore deposits, national environmental standards).

Instead of innovative new technologies that could contribute to a comparative advantage, most technological advances in the industry have been incremental—stepwise improvements of existing equipment and processes— rather than major breakthroughs. Incremental advances are certainly beneficial, but they may not be sufficient in the face of strong foreign competition based substantially on nontechnological factors. In such an environment, breakthrough technologies are needed (i.e., discontinuous advances that allow the domestic industry to capture sizable gains by applying entirely new technology) while competitors attempt to wrest incremental improvements from existing technology.

Industrial laboratories and research staffs in most of the minerals and metals companies have been cut back substantially and in some cases eliminated. Similarly, suppliers to the industry often cannot afford the research needed to develop new products. Because of the relative health of the U.S. industry at present, there is a widespread perception among industry managers that further advances in technology are (at least temporarily) less urgent. As a result, industry has limited interest in the adaptation and application of technologies derived from research performed by government or academe.

Much of the industry's lost R&D capabilities would be difficult and costly to restore in their original form. Collaborative research, particularly in the development of a shared technology base, could yield better results in terms of the competitiveness of the industry. Regardless of the form, however, a strong domestic capability for generating and applying technology is indispensable for future competitiveness. The industry itself must play the lead role in restoring and maintaining its ability to develop, receive, and implement new technologies.

Academe

The academic infrastructure for research and education in support of the minerals and metals industry has declined substantially over the past decade. Research programs are generally small, poorly funded, narrow in focus, and directed at incremental advances, thereby limiting the capability of colleges and universities to perform basic research leading to useful new technologies for minerals and metals production.

Student enrollments (both graduate and undergraduate), degrees, and the number of programs and faculty have all declined by large margins, and the survival of several programs is in doubt. The supply of B.S. graduates (especially those who are U.S. citizens) appears to be lower than current industry demand. If present trends continue, colleges and universities will be unable to meet the industry's need for well-trained engineering personnel to solve future problems.

Government

Historically, government and academic laboratories have made many significant contributions to the research base for minerals and metals, while industry has focused more intently on the application of research results to operational and site-specific projects. In response to low metal prices and intense foreign competition, the R&D focus of many companies has become even more near term in scope. At the same time, federal support for research, both at government and university laboratories, has declined.

The Mining and Minerals Policy Act of 1970 (P.L. 91-631) declared that it was the continuing policy of the United States to foster and encourage private enterprise in the development of a strong domestic mining, mineral, metal, and mineral reclamation industries. The State Mining and Minerals Resources Research Institute Program Act of 1984 (P.L. 98-409) calls for the Secretary of the Interior to perform, or verify the performance of, a number of functions that could greatly improve the competitive outlook of the U.S. minerals and metals industry. These functions, which would be implemented through the Bureau of Mines, include interagency coordination of mining and minerals research programs, interagency coordination and consolidation of data bases for the purpose of indicative planning, cataloging of all current and projected federally funded research relating to mining and mineral resources, and development of a national plan for research in these fields by a Committee on Mining and Mineral Resources Research. To date, these functions have not been performed in any consistent or deliberate way. Indeed, the Department of the Interior does not provide strong support for the Bureau's interests and programs.

The partnership between industry, academe, and government has weakened in the past several decades to a point where the pipeline of basic research in areas critical to the future competitiveness of the industry is drying up. The committee found that the mining and minerals research conducted by the government and in universities is not well coordinated with the long-term needs of industry. This situation must change; it is the basic research of today that will be the foundation for the technologies of tomorrow and that will support the strong domestic minerals and metals industry envisioned by the Mining and Minerals Policy Act. The Department of the Interior and the Bureau of Mines in particular are well situated to improve the research base for industry by rebuilding the collaboration in mining and minerals R&D. In addition to conducting research in its own laboratories and directing research funds to academic institutions, the Bureau can foster communication and collaboration among researchers to improve the applicability and timeliness of research.

Bureau of Mines

The Bureau of Mines has been and remains the only federal agency concerned primarily with the needs of the minerals and metals industry. Bureau support of R&D relevant to the needs of the industry contributed substantially to its growth and competitiveness throughout much of this century, particularly in the early decades. However, the Bureau's technological contributions have had less impact in recent years. Its R&D budget was lower in 1989 (even before inflation is taken into account) than it was in 1980. Some 40 to 50 percent of the Bureau's research is devoted to mine safety, health, and environmental protection, further limiting the funds available for technology to improve productivity.

The federal government can play an important role in helping the U.S. minerals and metals industry maintain a strong competitive posture internationally. The Bureau of Mines is presently the only federal agency positioned to provide that assistance. If the Bureau is to play a more active and effective role it will need to collaborate more closely with academe and industry.

Government-Academic-Industrial Cooperation

Both the 32 Mining and Minerals Resources Research Institutes (Mineral Institutes) and the 6 Generic Mineral Technology Centers (GMTCs) located at colleges and universities could be quite valuable for supplying the U.S. industry with well-trained manpower and technological advances. However, increasing their value will require stronger support, coordination of the research efforts within broad targets for research, a more critical approach to the selection and evaluation of projects, and elimination of less successful efforts in favor of promising new ones.

The Mineral Institutes and GMTCs are not well supported by the federal government. They are poorly funded, which hampers their ability to educate students and to perform needed research. The GMTCs suffer from a lack of strategic planning and rigorous evaluation of their research programs. Proposals funded under both of these programs tend to reflect the interests of researchers rather than the needs of the industry.

The relationship between government and industry in minerals and metals issues has often been an adversarial one. A variety of restrictions (antitrust, environmental, etc.) have been placed on the minerals industry with little or no consultation or involvement with industry experts. At the same time, however, the technology-forcing aspects of environmental regulations have sometimes forced companies to become more productive, albeit at heavy capital costs.

Foreign mineral producers generally work more closely with their governments in negotiating trade, environmental, and other policies. Indeed, the involvement of foreign governments has sometimes provided their industry with a competitive advantage in the international market through such policies that recognize the interests of their minerals and metals industry. The interests of the U.S. minerals and metals industry, on the other hand, are not represented in many governmental decisions on tax, trade, environmental, and other relevant policies. Closer relationships are being forged between the U.S. government and industry in the highly visible high-technology fields but not in the minerals and metals field.

In order to strengthen the international competitiveness of the domestic industry, a new and more positive relationship is needed between agencies of the U.S. government and the minerals and metals industry. Collaborative efforts are needed to develop technology for waste minimization, reduction of environmental impact, and remediation of contaminated waste sites. Government and industry should work together productively as partners to explore other research needs and should establish better communication links on policy issues. All concerned should recognize that some of our international competitors do not impose such heavy burdens or else they subsidize the producers who must implement them.

RECOMMENDED ACTIONS

The committee believes that the following recommended actions for industry, academe, and government can make a significant contribution to the long-term economic health of the domestic minerals and metals industry. Industry commitment is essential to the development and maintenance of a technology-based competitive advantage, but there are essential roles for academics and government as well. In particular, the Bureau of Mines has a key role to play in the conduct of research and the gathering and dissemination of information. Actions by any individual party will not be sufficient; to be effective all three groups must act in concert. The Bureau should be a leader in the development of a coordinated effort by government, industry, and academe to maintain and improve the competitiveness of the industry.

Industry must make greater use of the opportunities for collaborative research. Existing industry associations are underutilized and deserve greater support as a mechanism for conducting research. Opportunities for establishing research consortia to pursue basic research should be examined in light of changes made over the past decade in the laws and regulations guiding such consortia.

Academic research must address basic scientific and engineering problems of the mining and metals industry. Universities must seek funding from different sources in order to assure stability for long-term research. The federal government must contribute to this stability by committing to support funding of university research through the Mineral Institutes and the GMTCs. Academic programs must not be conducted in isolation; greater coordination among university researchers and greater collaboration between academe and industry are necessary. The Bureau of Mines should take a lead role in promoting coordination among government-supported research institutions and in facilitating the transfer of technology from research to industry.

The Bureau must increase its emphasis on productivity, not at the expense of its other research responsibilities but in synergy with them. Research should be pursued in areas that would provide a base for a national comparative advantage, emphasizing domestic strengths such as an educated work force and geological features that are unique to or more commonly located in the United States. Topics of high priority include the study of ore genesis and deposition, in situ mining, intelligent mining systems, and improved energy efficiency in processing. In addition, research on safety, health, and the environment will be of greater benefit to the United States, with its stricter environmental regulations, than to its competitors.

The Bureau should make a substantial commitment to conducting basic and exploratory research on "breakthrough" technologies that could contribute to competitiveness and to safety, health, and environmental concerns. This research should address new concepts with the potential to revolutionize the entire process from mining to metals extraction, and it should have a long-range focus on high-risk, high-payoff topics. This work should be coordinated with other Bureau research but should be programmatically separate.

The Bureau's commitment to information and analysis must be continued and strengthened. Emphasis should be placed on the dissemination of data and analysis, and opportunities for electronic access should be pursued. The Secretary of the Interior should promote the inclusion of the Bureau in interagency groups that address issues related to minerals and metals, notably matters of international trade, national security, and environmental protection.

The Bureau must increase its activity in the broader research community. It must actively support the Mineral Institutes and GMTCs and must work with academic researchers to focus research on topics that contribute to long-term national interests. The Bureau should also encourage the involvement of industry associations in defining goals and opportunities for academic research. In order to facilitate the role of the Bureau, the administration should support requests for funding of the Mineral Institutes and GMTCs rather than waiting for Congress to act.

The Bureau should seek outside advice on the direction and quality of its programs. An advisory committee established under the Public Advisory Committee Act should be established to advise the director on the direction and content of Bureau programs, including information needs, industry needs and opportunities, advances in technology, and priorities. In addition, visiting committees should be established to review the quality and content of the internal research programs of the Bureau, providing their advice to the research directors of the Bureau's laboratories and to the director.

A national minerals and metals community forum should be convened regularly to identify major technical and policy problems facing the industry. This forum will increase communication between representatives of industry, academe, and government as well as foster collaboration among these groups. In order for the domestic minerals and metals industry to survive, there must be long-term commitment to a continuing reevaluation of the problems and opportunities facing the industry.

1

U.S. Minerals and Metals Industry in a Changing Global Context

WORLD MINERALS AND METALS INDUSTRY

Globalization of Production and Ownership

Mineral exploration in the United States began in earnest in about 1850, leading to the discovery of some of the world's richest deposits of many major minerals. High-grade iron ore, copper, gold, and silver deposits were plentiful. Lead and zinc deposits were extensive, and their relatively low grades were offset by proximity to burgeoning markets. By the latter decades of the nineteenth century, however, growth in worldwide demand began to stimulate interest in global exploration. Gold was among the first targets, responding to concern that U.S. deposits could not fulfill the needs of the industrial economies of both North America and Europe. British and U.S. firms opened new gold mines in South Africa, Australia, and Latin America. By the turn of the century, base metals were being mined in Canada, Australia, and Mexico. By the beginning of World War I, several large copper projects were operating in Chile and central Africa, and rich lead, zinc, and silver ores were flowing from Peru.

Most sectors of the U.S. industry were still growing vigorously during this period of internationalization. Producers compensated for declining ore grades through economies of scale and technological advancements. By 1920 open pit mines served by steam shovels had become the rule in iron ore and copper, and electrically driven equipment was being introduced in the larger underground mines. The flotation process, invented in England

and first exploited in Australia, was almost universally employed. Electrorefining of zinc had been developed at Anaconda by 1913, and copper electrowinning, which originated in the United States, was being installed in Chile. All in all, these advances were building a U.S. lead in scale and technology that was not to be seriously challenged until after 1945.

World War II greatly accelerated the depletion of higher-grade ore reserves in the United States and Canada. The United States began a 20-year period of economic growth, consuming minerals and metals at rates that threatened to outstrip U.S. production and make the nation partly dependent on imports for major metal ores. Geologists and engineers, primarily from the United States but also from Europe and Canada, fanned out across the world to find new deposits and build new mines and plants. Much of the new foreign production was consumed by the recovery and rebuilding in Europe and Japan, so it did not challenge the traditional markets of the established U.S. minerals and metals companies. Because U.S. firms owned or controlled many of the foreign producers, moreover, there was a sense that, even if growth were to slow, U.S. interests would be protected.

The international transformation that affected the U.S. minerals and metals industry occurred over a period of many decades. U.S. financial involvement focused initially on Canada and Mexico, but investors eventually became involved in the South African and Australian gold fields, the Chilean copper mines, and other areas. By the end of World War II, the U.S. companies had joined British and other European investors in the domination of world mineral production.

While some companies emerged to exploit specific deposits or areas (e.g., Cyprus Mines in Cyprus and Cerro de Pasco Corporation in Peru), many entered the international field from a strong domestic base (Anaconda, ASARCO, Kennecott, and Newmont were typical). At the same time, however, many major companies such as Phelps Dodge, New Jersey Zinc, and St. Joe Minerals remained almost entirely domestic until the 1960s or later.

When U.S. companies did become involved overseas, their style was ownership—often total and almost always controlling. Many U.S.-owned facilities maintained large expatriate staffs, and their operations were usually sheltered by very favorable taxation and profit repatriation rules. However, growing nationalism in developing countries, combined with an interest in a larger share of the benefits of their natural resources, led them to increase national control of their basic mineral resources. Most foreign-owned copper mines in the Third World had been expropriated by the early 1970s, either wholly or in part. Iron ore and bauxite followed a similar course, with output passing into the hands of government-controlled entities. Lead and zinc were less affected, many because the mines and smelters were concentrated in developed countries such as Canada, Australia, and the United States itself.

Changing Patterns of Supply and Demand

By itself the wave of nationalizations would have had relatively little effect on the competitive positions of U.S. domestic producers, since most of the Third World output was already flowing to markets in the developed countries. However, these events roughly coincided with the energy crisis of 1973 and the recession that followed. Increased energy costs drove mining and processing costs upward. Metals and minerals prices increased at first but then declined as the demand for metals dropped with the onset of recession (see Figure 1-1). Burdened with debt and the need for foreign exchange, Third World producers struggled to maximize output despite lower demand. Commercial banks and multilateral lending agencies, eager to

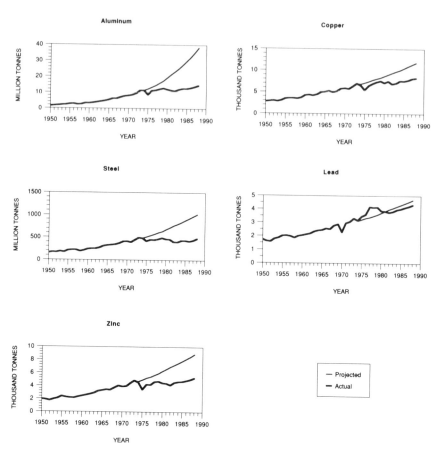

FIGURE 1-1 Actual and projected growth of consumption of various metals: Western world, 1950-1988.

recycle petrodollars, continued to lend for new projects. At about the same time, U.S. mining and metals companies, believing that reduced demand was a temporary condition of the recession, continued to invest heavily in new expensive efforts to exploit marginal resources—adding still more supply toward the higher ends of the cost curves. Petroleum companies, seeking expansion opportunities for the increased income generated by rising oil prices, bought major minerals and metals companies and supported their expansion plans.

Meanwhile, demand for metals remained depressed after the recession in 1975, even when the world economy recovered. One factor was the end of the Vietnam War, but another important reason for stagnant demand was a declining intensity of use for these materials (Table 1-1). Intensity of use (I/U) is defined as the amount of a given mineral or metal consumed in producing a unit of the gross national product (GNP). That is, after the mid-1970s the use of primary metals in the developed nations began to drop sharply through a combination of downsizing (e.g., of automobiles), conservation (e.g., recycling of aluminum cans), and substitution by other materials (e.g., plastics in everything from telephones to trucks).

TABLE 1-1 Average Annual Change in Western World Metals Consumption, Gross Domestic Product, and Intensity of Use, 1960–1973 and 1973–1986

Metal and Period	Average Annual Change (%)		
	Metal Consumption	Gross Domestic Product	Intensity of Use
Aluminum			
1960–1973	9.9	5.2	4.5
1973–1986	1.3	2.7	−1.4
Copper			
1960–1973	4.6	5.2	−0.6
1973–1986	0.8	2.7	−1.8
Steel			
1960–1973	5.6	5.2	0.4
1973–1986	−1.1	2.7	−3.7
Zinc			
1960–1973	5.4	5.2	0.1
1973–1986	0.0	2.	-2

SOURCES: Metal consumption data are from Metall (annual) and International Iron and Steel Institute; GDP data are from the World Bank.

Metal demand was recovering in the late 1970s until the oil market was again shaken by the actions in the Middle East and the Organization of Petroleum Exporting Countries (OPEC) in 1979. The threat of rising energy costs further depressed demand. Third World metal producers, faced with pressing economic demands and limited sources of capital, again tried to increase production despite stagnating demand. This policy kept prices low, which in turn increased their financial burdens, leading to further overproduction. Overproduction and excess capacity caused a major shift in the economics of metals and minerals. Industry pleas for government intervention could not be heeded without raising consumer prices and risking a banking crisis or worse in some countries. While some help was given—most notably to steel via trigger pricing and voluntary restraint agreements—the U.S. government generally took a hands-off approach. It was only by the second half of the 1980s that growth of demand and declining investment into new capacity brought the market in balance at higher metal prices.

The United States, traditionally the dominant market for minerals and metals in absolute terms, had also been a leader in the increasing intensity of their use during the first half of the century. This began to change markedly after World War II. Even Europe and Japan, with their postwar reconstruction completed, have seen their intensity of metals use decline. It has come to be accepted that, as a developed society's standard of living rises, its per capita demand for minerals and metals drops (Malenbaum, 1978). In developing nations, on the other hand, demand increases as they build housing, factories, schools, and infrastructure, which are already in place in developed nations. In some cases developing nations are able to develop indigenous sources of supply, but in many cases they must import minerals and metals they lack or cannot produce efficiently.

This growth in demand in the Third World may eventually provide a large market for minerals and metals but not for many years to come. First, even strong growth from a low base can take a long time to reach a significant level in global terms. For example, a 10 percent increase in Brazilian copper consumption would be required to offset a 1.1 percent decline in U.S. copper use (World Bureau of Metal Statistics, 1989). Second, developing countries frequently lack the foreign exchange needed to purchase the metals and minerals they need. While the developing countries may eventually become major consumers, industrialized nations, in short, will remain the major end-use markets for the foreseeable future.

Changing Corporate Structure of the Industry

At mid-century the United States was a dominant producer as well as a major market for minerals; three or four American companies, with their

British and European counterparts, virtually controlled price and supply in most mineral sectors. These large companies specialized in one mineral and its coproducts (where different minerals occurred in a single ore body). They also tended to be vertically integrated, mining and processing the ores into metal and in some cases (particularly in the aluminum industry) continuing their operations even further downstream into the fabrication of consumer items.

The corporate structure of the world minerals and metals industry has changed enormously over the past quarter-century. There are now many more players in many more countries throughout the world. Full vertical integration is now much less common, particularly in the base metal industries: the former giants have in many cases shrunk, disappeared, or divested their interests to concentrate on one phase of activity (mining, processing, or fabrication). In addition, those companies have spread their risks by diversifying into different metals, nonmetallic materials, and even energy and other types of products. Most of the largest companies today are multinational, multimetal holding companies comprised of independent subsidiaries.

TRENDS IN THE U.S. INDUSTRY

A recent study by the Congressional Research Service (CRS) reported that "the United States is no longer the world's leading producer of most metals. It now functions within the framework of the total world market rather than in isolation or as a dominant force" (CRS, 1986, p. 5). Management and technical superiority once gave U.S. companies strong advantages over their competitors. As ore grades have diminished, however, it has become increasingly difficult to maintain a strong position in the market based solely on management and incremental technical advances. Foreign industries have learned our management techniques, and technology now crosses borders more fluidly than ever before. Many factors external to the activities of mining, processing, and fabricating metals have also worked to the disadvantage of the U.S. industry. For example, the cost of complying with federal environmental regulations is about 6 cents per pound of lead and between 9 and 15 cents per pound of copper—about 20 percent of the price of each metal in 1986, though rising metal prices have reduced this fraction to more like 10 percent today; the added cost for many other nations with less stringent environmental restrictions is far lower.

The condition of the domestic industry in 1984 was bleak, prompting a *Business Week* cover story entitled "The death of mining" (Houston et al., 1984). The industry had failed to rebound from the recession that ended in 1982: prices remained low in the face of foreign overproduction, and profitability continued to decline despite the general recovery felt in other sectors of the economy. Labor costs were among the highest in the world, and the strong dollar made imported metals more attractive than domestic products. During the late 1970s and early 1980s, major oil companies had bought up mining companies but were then (for the most part) unable to operate them profitably. Buyouts, layoffs, and plant closings became commonplace as the industry retrenched. Figure 1-2 shows this retrenchment graphically in the form of falling market shares.

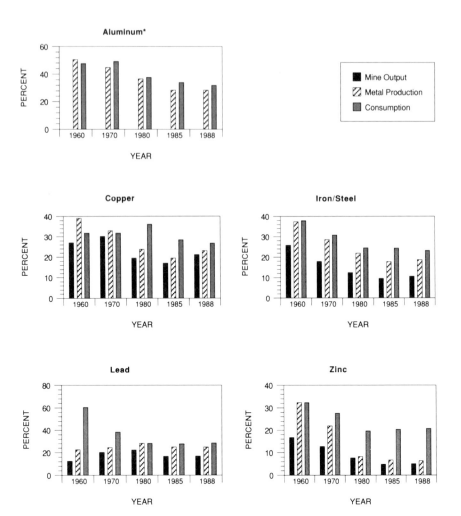

* There is virtually no domestic production of bauxite, so there is no column for mine production of aluminum.

FIGURE 1-2 U.S. mine output, metal production, and consumption of selected metals as a percentage of Western world.

By 1985 the domestic nonferrous metals industry had recorded four consecutive years of heavy losses. Prices (in constant dollar terms) of several major metals had reached their lowest level since the Great Depression (Figure 1-3). Copper, which was then the largest of the domestic nonferrous minerals industries in terms of employment and total earnings, was especially hard hit. Domestic copper mines were satisfying less than 60 percent of total domestic demand, and domestic smelting and refining operations fared even less well. In 1983, with the price of copper falling below 70 cents per pound, no integrated U.S. copper operation was able to break even on its operating costs (CRS, 1986, p. 15). Even aluminum producers, who had traditionally been more profitable than other sectors of the metals industry, experienced losses of 30 cents per pound in 1982 and 19 cents per pound in 1984 (CRS, 1986, p. 106).

The iron ore mining industry, which contributes about the same amount to the U.S. GNP as does the copper mining industry, also experienced severe contraction during the 1981-1982 recession. Capacity utilization in 1982 was around 40 percent, less than half the 1979 peak. Due to pronounced integration of the domestic iron and steel industry, however, domestic iron ore prices remained more stable than other ore prices. For example, in the 1979-1983 period, real domestic prices of lead, copper, and zinc declined by 68 percent, 37 percent, and 15 percent, respectively, compared to 10 percent or less for iron ore pellets (CRS, 1986, p. 73).

The U.S. molybdenum industry is the world's largest, with approximately half of the world's known resources. Because it is a high-value product, the value of U.S. molybdenum mine production in most years is twice that of

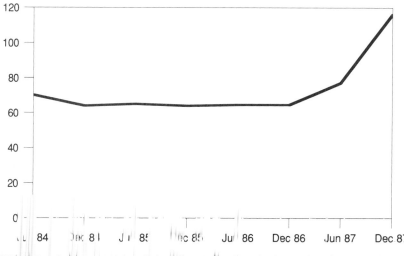

FIGURE 1-3 Metals price index. Source: Bureau of Mines, the Mineral Position of the United States—1988.

the lead and zinc output, ranking third in total value behind copper and iron ore. Along with gold, it is one of only two metallic minerals that the United States still exports in large amounts. Nevertheless, due to sustained worldwide overproduction and low prices, the domestic primary molybdenum industry also experienced large losses, layoffs, and plant closings throughout the 1980s. By-product molybdenum, on the other hand, has thrived along with copper.

Lead is the fourth-largest domestic metal industry, based on mine production. The U.S. lead industry is the world's largest producer. Although domestic ore grades are low compared to foreign deposits, domestic producer costs are fairly low and output is efficient. The U.S. lead industry, restructured after the recession of the early 1980s, performed well in the late 1980s. U.S. lead production is unusual in that, for over 90 percent of the mines, lead is the dominant product; elsewhere, lead ordinarily occurs as a secondary coproduct with zinc and other metals.

Fifth in terms of its market value is the zinc mining industry. Due to low ore grades, a relative absence of coproducts in U.S. zinc deposits, and low world zinc prices, the health of the domestic zinc industry has declined sharply since the 1960s—more so than in the copper, lead, or iron ore industries. The decline has been seen across the board, at mines, smelters, and refineries. Smelting and refining capacity was cut nearly in half between 1975 and 1985. By 1986 domestic mine output of zinc was the lowest in 80 years and metal production was the lowest in 50 years (Bureau of Mines, 1987, p. 28). Owing to its poor reserve base, domestic zinc is unlikely to mount a strong recovery.

For steel, aluminum, and the base metals, the second half of the 1980s marked a general improvement over the first. Other domestic mining and metals industries have had different experiences in recent years. Titanium, for example, increased steadily in both production and consumption throughout the 1980s, in part because of the U.S. defense buildup but largely because its highest-volume use is as titanium dioxide in paint pigment. Employment has held steady and prices have trended slightly upward. Even exports have been steady, at about 13 percent of production (Bureau of Mines, 1989, p. 172). But in the high-value sponge metal, domestic production has dropped while imports have risen. U.S. production of titanium sponge fell 25 percent in 1986 alone and was at about 55 percent of capacity by the end of that year (Bureau of Mines, 1987, p. 29).

By contrast, the precious-metals industries have remained strong domestically as gold and silver have generally held their price or risen in value. New gold mines opened at a rapid rate: over 40 in 1986, 37 in 1987, and 36 in 1988. Domestic mine production of gold increased by about 172 percent between 1985 and 1988 (Bureau of Mines, 1987, p. 64). Soon there will be more silver produced as a coproduct of gold mining than by direct silver mining in the United States. The economics of gold and silver are much simpler than those of other metals: although profitability is keyed to price, price in turn is largely keyed to factors other than supply.

REVIVAL OF THE MINERALS AND METALS INDUSTRY

At the end of 1985 the situation for most of the domestic mining and minerals industry was grim, but in 1986 demand increased and prices for metals soon rose, sometimes dramatically. Losses eased, turning into profits for many companies. As this improvement continued into 1987 and 1988, the turnaround became obvious (see Table 1-2). In 1988 the overall value

TABLE 1-2 U.S. Production of Selected Metals, 1983–1989 (million metric tons, except as noted)

	1983	1984	1985	1986	1987	1988	1989
FERROUS METALS							
Iron ore	38.2	52.1	49.5	39.5	47.6	57.5	58.7
Iron and steel, 10^6 short ton							
Pig iron	48.8	52.0	50.0	44.3	48.3	55.7	53.8
Steel and cast iron	84.6	92.5	88.3	81.6	89.2	99.9	96.7
NONFERROUS METALS							
Aluminum							
Primary	3.4	4.1	3.5	3.0	3.3	3.9	4.0
Secondary	0.8	0.8	0.9	0.8	0.9	1.0	1.1
Copper							
Mine	1.0	1.1	1.1	1.1	1.3	1.4	1.5
Refinery[a]	1.6	1.5	1.4	1.5	1.6	1.9	2.0
Copper from old scrap	0.4	0.5	0.5	0.5	0.5	0.5	0.5
Gold, 10^6 troy ounce							
Mine	2.0	2.1	2.4	3.7	5.0	6.6	7.8
Refinery[a]	7.1	5.4	5.2	5.6	7.0	8.6	10.4
Lead							
Mine	0.5	0.4	0.4	0.4	0.3	0.4	0.5
Refinery[a]	1.0	1.0	1.1	0.9	1.0	1.1	1.1
Titanium, 10^3 metric tons							
Metal	12.7	22.1	21.1	16.8	17.8	22.2	24.0
Titanium dioxide	691	758	783	844	879	926	1007
Zinc							
Mine	0.2	0.2	0.2	0.2	0.2	0.2	0.3

[a] Primary and secondary.

SOURCE: Bureau of Mines, Mineral Commodity Summaries 1989.

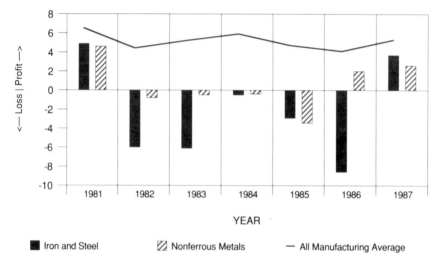

FIGURE 1-4 Profit and loss trends in the domestic metals industries, 1981-1987. Source: Bureau of Mines.

of raw minerals production in the United States had nearly doubled compared to 1986, from $5.8 billion to $10.4 billion. Figure 1-4 depicts the strongly improved profitability of the industry as a whole in 1987. Profits have continued to improve, gaining an average of 73 percent in the first quarter of 1989 (Atchison et al., 1989) but easing in the fourth quarter.

Factors Leading to the Recovery

Several factors, some internal to the industry and others external, converged to create the revival in minerals and metals. One factor was the range of adjustments that the industries had made internally in response to stringent economic conditions. Plant closings led to capacity reductions, while rationalization of mining operations reduced costs. Further cost reductions were achieved by reducing labor costs through both layoffs and wage reductions and by broadening the scope of many union jobs to increase flexibility and reduce personnel requirements. From 1981 to 1989, North American metals mining companies cut employment in half, helping to raise their productivity by as much as sixfold (Atchison et al., 1989). Restructuring and changes in mine and plant ownership reduced management costs and brought in fresh capital. Negotiations with utility authorities led in many cases to reduced energy costs, while greater energy efficiency was also sought. In the aluminum industry, for example, overall efficiency of energy use increased by 22 percent between 1976 and 1986 (Bureau of Mines, 1987, p.

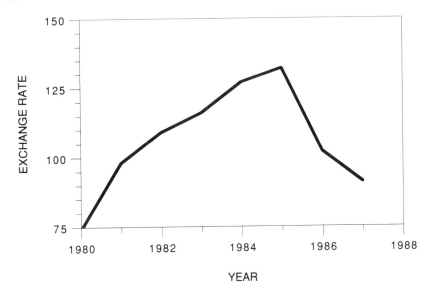

FIGURE 1-5 Exchange value of the dollar, 1980-1987. Source: Federal Reserve Board.

10). Productivity and profitability were improved not only by restructuring but also through greater use of lower-cost, more efficient technologies such as solvent extraction and electrowinning in copper from suitable ores. By such means several copper companies stemmed their losses even before prices began to rise.

Second, demand for most metals grew sharply in 1986, largely in response to a continued economic recovery that by then had spread beyond the United States. At the same time, worldwide supply constraints began to be felt in copper, aluminum, lead, and zinc (Bureau of Mines, 1987, p. 28). Reduced levels of investment in new projects throughout the world, combined with higher demand, resulted in a better balance between capacity and expected future demand.

Third, the dollar weakened against most other major currencies, reducing relative domestic costs of production and making domestic products more attractive to domestic and many foreign consumers alike (see Figure 1-5). This also benefited foreign producers of nonfuel minerals--Canada, Australia, and the Third World—as the lower prices in other currencies encouraged increased consumption. Overall the weak dollar helped with some metals such as copper, gaining more than others.

Effects of the Recovery

In the first half of the decade capacity utilization in the minerals and metals industry had generally fallen, followed by cuts in capacity via closures and rationalization. Once the recovery got under way, capacity utilization quickly rose to optimum levels in most cases.

The recovery has aided several of the individual metal industries, probably none more so than copper. Essentially, the U.S. copper industry had the best resource base and took the most drastic measures during the early 1980s to cut costs and increase productivity. Due to cost-cutting measures and new technologies, and to a lesser extent the decline of the dollar, costs for U.S. producers have fallen sharply relative to costs for many foreign producers (see Figure 1-6). The average cost of copper production fell from 79 cents per pound in 1981 to 54 cents per pound in 1986. With consumption rising and copper inventories at a 12-year low in mid-1986, copper prices began trending upward from a base of 60 cents to 64 cents per pound (OTA, 1988). By late 1987 the average price was well over 80 cents per pound, and U.S. copper producers were profitable again.

The U.S. lead industry came back almost as strongly as copper. During 1987 and 1988 lead mine and metal production both increased, reversing the trend of the previous years, although production remained below the levels of 1979. The average world lead price rose 62 percent between April

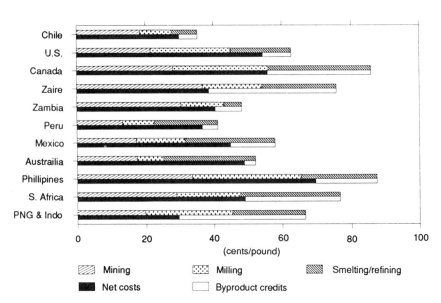

FIGURE 1-6 Copper production costs—United States versus rest of Western world.

and July 1987 alone. The U.S. lead industry has not enjoyed unequivocal improvement, however; demand for lead has been falling because of environmental regulations and reduced lead content in gasoline. The U.S. industry has seen sharp reductions in primary capacity in recent years. Despite these reductions, primary refinery capacity utilization of the domestic lead industry was still only 60 percent in 1987, the lowest rate since 1968,

St. Joe Lead Mines, Missouri lead operations, circa 1870. (Courtesy N. Arbiter.)

The Viburnum Lead Mine in Southeast Missouri, 1989. (Courtesy The Doe Run Company.)

while the utilization rate in the secondary sector has risen to almost 90 percent, the highest ever recorded (Bureau of Mines, 1988, p. 30). In 1986 St. Joe Lead Company merged with the lead operations of Homestake Mining Company to form the Doe Run Company, representing two-thirds of the U.S. lead mining capacity and over one-half of its primary refined lead capacity (Bureau of Mines, 1987, p. 28). Reduced and rationalized capacity, along with a weaker dollar, has helped bring the lead industry back to modest profitability.

Zinc consumption worldwide set two successive records in 1986 and 1987 before falling off slightly in 1988. Mine and metal production also reached record highs in 1987. Reflecting the high demand, prices for zinc also rose sharply after April 1987 (Porter, 1988). Domestic mine and metal output also increased in 1987 and 1988, with new mine openings and two reopenings. With the fall in the dollar, domestic producer prices made a stronger advance than those on the London Metal Exchange. Nevertheless, the domestic zinc industry continued to contract.

The aluminum industry has evolved differently than the base metal industries. Both capacity and production of primary aluminum in the United States declined steadily through the mid-1980s. Conditions began to improve in early 1987, as prices rose sharply along with export orders, and some previously closed plants were reopened on a temporary basis. The price for primary aluminum increased by well over 50 percent during 1987. In response, primary aluminum production grew by about 5 percent in 1987, and capacity utilization rose from 72 to 90 percent (Bureau of Mines, 1988, p. 30). However, overall domestic capacity did not increase. A major problem was the cost of energy relative to energy costs in the rest of the world. In the long term the Bureau of Mines estimates that domestic aluminum production will probably account for only about 63 percent of U.S. demand for primary metal and 43 percent of U.S. industrial demand by the year 2000 (Bureau of Mines, 1987, p. 30).

The steel industry also participated in the recovery. World raw steel output in 1987 was the highest in 8 years, with stainless steel production increasing 9.3 percent over 1986 (Butler and Dopson, 1988). World steel production then increased again by some 7 percent in 1988 (Bureau of Mines, 1989, p. 83). Prices for steel products rose dramatically during 1987, but in 1988 they slipped back to the 1986 level. Overall, conditions for the domestic steel industry improved due to lower imports, strong demand, and the falling value of the dollar. U.S. raw steel output rose nearly 14 percent in 1988 due to both the competitive prices of domestic producers and the voluntary restraint agreements then in place. Demand for domestic steel grew, so that plants operated at well over 85 percent of capacity in 1988, a strong improvement over the 55 to 70 percent utilization rates of 1986. Most domestic steel producers reported profits, but plant closures and industry restructuring continued. However, the iron ore industry lagged behind the general improvement: 1986 was the second-worst year for U.S. iron ore production since 1939, although production increased by 25 percent from 1987 to 1988 as prices held steady. This occurred because much of the early improvement in steel came from scrap-based electric furnaces or "mini-mills."

Outlook for the Industry

Given the revival just described, the crucial question is whether the U.S. mining and minerals industry is out of danger. The prudent answer to that question must be *no*. Although recent economic trends have prevented extreme difficulties and turbulence in many sectors, not one of the domestic industries described above can be considered securely profitable. They have enjoyed a brief run of profitability after several years of debilitating losses, but there is no guarantee that this run will continue.

For example, many of the recent gains could be reversed rapidly by an increase in U.S. interest rates followed by a strengthening of the dollar. Another major recession combined with high world production could drop the price of copper, for example, by almost 50 percent. For most of these minerals and metals there are few remaining opportunities to cut costs. More fundamentally, the restructuring of the U.S. industry has left it unable to maintain a long-term dominance in any subindustry except perhaps molybdenum. U.S. producers are seeking opportunities for new investments, but they find it difficult to generate sufficient optimism to support real expansion. A range of environmental, financial, and management constraints, discussed in the following chapter, pose formidable disincentives.

The prospect is not for the "death" of the U.S. mining and minerals industry but rather for continued instability and vulnerability to world economic factors. The relatively sudden revival of prices and profitability during the latter half of the decade poses the danger of false hope. There is also a risk that the industry and the nation will be lulled into believing that the current situation signals a permanent return to prosperity for mining and minerals. In reality it is a welcome but temporary upward turn for an industry that in all likelihood will continue to face challenges to its place in the world market.

REFERENCES

Atchison, S. D., C. Hawkins, C. Schroeder, an I . / [in|. 198°. The mining industry climbs out of the pits. *Business W e k* J   ), |p 61-63.
Butler, T., and J. Dopson. 1988. Steel. In *Mii in ;.   l l e iew*, b. 57.
Bureau of Mines. 1987. *The Mineral Positio f h   ed St tes: Annual Report*

of the Secretary of the Interior Under the Mining and Minerals Policy Act of 1970. Washington, D.C.: U.S. Government Printing Office.

Bureau of Mines. 1988. *The Mineral Position of the United States*. Washington, D.C.: U.S. Government Printing Office.

Bureau of Mines. 1989. *Mineral Commodity Summaries*. Washington, D.C.: U.S. Government Printing Office.

Congressional Research Service (CRS). 1986. *The Competitiveness of American Metal Mining and Processing*. Report prepared for the U.S. House of Representatives, Committee on Energy and Commerce, Subcommittee on Oversight and Investigations. Committee Print 99-FF. Washington, D.C.: U.S. Government Printing Office.

Houston, P., Z. Schiller, S. D. Atchison, M. Crawford, J. R. Norman, R. James, and J. Ryser. 1984. The death of mining. *Business Week*, December 17, pp. 64-70.

Malenbaum, W. 1978. *World Demand for Raw Materials in 1985 and 2000*. New York: McGraw-Hill.

Office of Technology Assessment. 1988. *Copper: Technology & Competitiveness*. OTA-E-368. Washington, D.C.: U.S. Government Printing Office, p. 19.

Porter, F. C. 1988. Zinc. In *Mining Annual Review*, p. 35.

World Metal Statistics Yearbook. 1989. Ware, Hertshire, England. World Bureau of Metal Statistics.

2

Supply, Demand, and Competitiveness

OVERVIEW OF THE MINERALS AND METALS INDUSTRY

This chapter identifies actions, policies, and technologies that may help maintain or improve the competitiveness of the domestic minerals industry and focuses attention on five metal subindustries—aluminum, copper, lead, zinc, and steel—that represent three distinctly different situations. The U.S. aluminum industry, for example, is oriented to the production of alloys and specialized products; it depends on foreign production of bauxite and, increasingly, alumina and even aluminum metal. The producers of copper, lead, and zinc, on the other hand, concentrate on the mining of ore and the production of metal for sale in commodity markets. The steel industry is more oriented toward the processing of iron ore and scrap into steel alloys but not to the degree of specialization found in the aluminum industry. Together, these three different situations can provide insights into the range of issues faced by the domestic minerals and metals industry as a whole. The basic stages of exploration, mining, and processing are similar for every metal product (see Box), but the particular form of these stages differs from metal to metal, and each subindustry has developed a structure that reflects the production and consumption of its products. (See Chapter 3 for further discussion of these technologies.)

The world distribution of metal production and consumption reflects both the mineral endowments of the producer countries and the investment policies of mining firms and national governments. Leading mine producers are the developing nations in Africa and South America and large developed

OVERVIEW OF MINING AND METAL PRODUCTION PROCESSES

The process of locating mineral deposits is termed *exploration*. In the past, exploration was accomplished almost entirely by examination of surface topographical features and by the taking of core samples. While these methods are still employed today, they have been augmented by remote (e.g., seismic) analysis of deeper subterranean features, by analysis of photographic and spectrographic data collected from aircraft and even satellites, by computer modeling techniques, and even by biochemical analysis of organic material on the surface.

Mining is the process of removing ore from the ground, either by open pit or underground methods. The next phase, often termed *beneficiation*, involves the production of a form of the ore in which the mineral is more concentrated. This may be accomplished by physical means, in which the ore is reduced to smaller particles by mechanical crushing and grinding, followed by physical separation of the mineral values from the ore to produce a "concentrate"—material containing a relatively high percentage of the metal of interest. In other cases, the mineral values are leached out of the ore by chemical means, a process known as hydrometallurgy. Heap leaching, using a chemical as the leaching agent to extract a mineral such as gold from a pile of ore or tailings (waste materials from earlier mining), is one such method.

The products of physical separation and leaching are subjected to chemical separation using either low-temperature (hydrometallurgical) or high-temperature (pyrometallurgical) means to yield a metal of suitable purity. *Pyrometallurgical processing* involves a combination of heat and chemical or electrolytic treatment of the concentrates in a process known as smelting. The resulting metal may then be further purified by chemical and electrolytic "refining" techniques. Depending on the nature of the ore and the metal, both smelting and refining may consist of several discrete steps. *Hydrometallurgical processing* involves relatively newer techniques in which the mineral solutions resulting from leaching are subjected to either electrical or chemical treatment.

With either method (pyro- or hydrometallurgical), the end product is a purified metal that is then melted and cast into any of several forms convenient for use and/or transportation—ingots, bars, slabs, etc. In some cases processing is extended into the production of "semifabricated parts" such as sheets, tubing, and wire, from which more complex shapes or products can be manufactured by the end user.

The processing of many ores is complicated by the fact that they contain more than one metal of economic interest. This has major implications for the economics of the minerals and metals industry, since the "coproducts," while less plentiful in the ore, may in some cases be nearly as valuable as the primary mineral of interest. Copper mining produces substantial amounts of gold, silver, and molybdenum as coproducts; about 5 percent of all domestic gold production in 1988 was recovered through processing copper and other base metals.

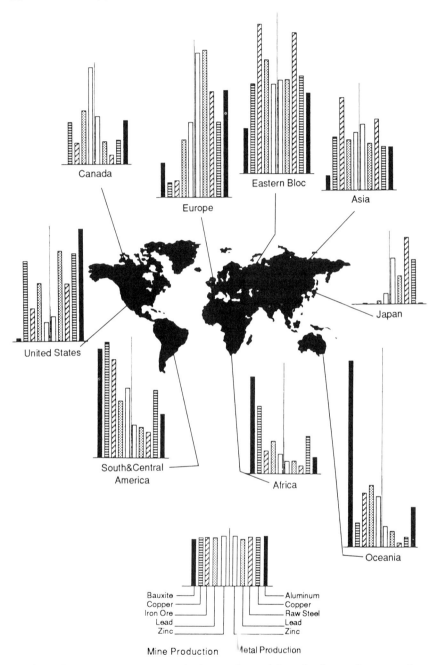

FIGURE 2-1 World distribution of mine output, metal production, and consumption.

TABLE 2-1 Categories of Metals

Base metals	Platinum group metals
Copper	Platinum
Lead	Palladium
Zinc	Rhodium
Tin	Ruthenium
Steel industry metals	Iridium
(iron and ferroalloys)	Osmium
Iron	**Precious metals**
Manganese	Gold
Nickel	Silver
Chromium	**Electronic materials**
Cobalt	Silicon
Molybdenum	Cadmium
Tungsten	Gallium
Vanadium	Germanium
Columbium	Selenium
Light metals	Tellurium
Aluminum	Tantalum
Lithium	Indium
Magnesium	Rhenium
Titanium	

countries, principally Australia, the United States, and Canada. While ores may be treated and processed near the mine, refining of metals and production of commodity products or specialty alloys takes place predominantly in the developed nations. This is illustrated in Figure 2-1, which shows the distribution of production and consumption of the five subject metals for the United States and other regions of the world. Current global trade patterns are the product of a gradual evolution, as mineral resource bases, technologies, politics, and economics have slowly changed throughout the world.

The subindustries are generally categorized according to type of metal, as shown in Table 2-1. The base metals—copper, lead, and zinc—have long comprised a substantial market. Iron ore, pig iron, and steel together comprise an enormous industry worldwide; they are usually considered as a single category, separate from the nonferrous metals. The steel industry metals, often referred to as ferroalloys—manganese, chromium, cobalt, molybdenum, nickel, tungsten, vanadium, and columbium—are those that are commonly combined with steel to make alloys having special properties as well as being used in their unalloyed metallic form.

Another category consists of the light metals—aluminum, lithium, magnesium, and titanium. These are metals that because of their high strength, low weight, and other special properties have replaced steel for some uses over the past century and particularly in recent decades. Aluminum is the second most widely used metal in the world. Magnesium and titanium, by contrast, are high-value materials with relatively small annual world production levels. Lithium is used in small amounts as an element in new aluminum alloys that have high strength-to-weight ratio, but these alloys are not yet in wide commercial use.

The precious metals comprise a separate category. Although these metals have important industrial uses, they are also traded for investment purposes

The platinum metals are similar to precious metals in that they have an investment purpose, but they are also used as catalysts in chemical reactions and for pollution control purposes.

The newest category of metals is termed electronic materials, a reference to the role they play in the computer and communications industries and other electronic applications such as batteries and switches. The category includes silicon, cadmium, gallium, germanium, selenium, tellurium, tantalum, indium, and rhenium. With the exception of silicon, the electronic minerals and metals are relatively scarce. They often occur in combination with other more common metals and are produced as by-products of the mining and refining of those metals.

TRENDS IN MINERAL AND METAL PRODUCTION

Aluminum

Aluminum is produced in a two-stage process: the raw ore, bauxite, is converted into alumina, the principal oxide of aluminum, which is then smelted to produce aluminum metal. The two stages are independent and can therefore be located at different sites. Bauxite is mined in over a dozen countries, with much of the ore located in the equatorial latitudes. Bauxite is often processed into alumina near the deposit, reducing the amount of material to be shipped and allowing the host country to share in the value added by processing. Since the production of aluminum from alumina is a highly energy-intensive process, the availability and cost of electricity are major factors in the siting of smelting facilities.

For many years sufficient electrical capacity was available only in the industrialized countries. This began to change in the 1970. As petroleum prices rose, so did the cost of electricity, causing dramatic changes in the economics of aluminum production. One result is that future smelters are likely to be located outside the United States, probably closer to the mine site. The U.S. aluminum industry previously had the competitive advantage of low-cost electric power, but now such countries as Brazil and Canada are capable of providing electricity at prices that are low relative to those charged in the United States.

The U.S. aluminum industry will retain other advantages resulting from low-cost transportation on inland waterways and proximity to markets as well as a base of existing facilities. Because aluminum smelting is capital intensive, existing smelters can continue to compete with new smelters in other countries. Finally, the aluminum industry extends far downstream to include the production of specialty alloys in forms desired by the consumer. Firms in the aluminum industry compete not only on metal price and production costs but also on the ability to deliver desired products.

After several decades of expansion, however, it appears that domestic production of aluminum has peaked. Due in large part to the high cost of electric power in the United States, it is unlikely that there will be significant investment in new domestic aluminum plants. As the cost of operating domestic smelters increases due to increases in domestic energy costs or other factors such as fitting pollution control systems to existing facilities, even the current level of domestic smelting capacity is likely to decline. The U.S. aluminum industry will likely remain strong because it is vertically integrated and can combine investment in overseas mines and processing facilities with domestic alloy production and production of semifabricated products.

Steel

The huge steel industry has evolved into two independent components. Once dominated by large integrated facilities, the industry is now segmented into "mini-mills," which rely on scrap steel for input and produce basic steel as an output, and large facilities that continue to produce raw steel, both for processing into semifabricated products and for further processing into specialty alloys.

The industry's raw materials—iron ore and scrap steel—are commodities that can be obtained from a variety of sources. As a result the competitive basis for the steel industry depends less on the cost of raw materials and more on the costs of processing them into steel and steel products. To a greater degree than the base metals, steel has some specialized markets where a firm can compete based on the quality of the marketed product.

Base Metals

Base metals—copper, lead, and zinc—are commodity products. The bulk of production is processed into standard forms, such as wire, slab, ingot or billet, and sold either on contract or through commodity exchanges. These products are produced to meet consumer standards, and to the degree that the products meet those standards, price is the principal measure of competition.

Copper

Over the past four decades the copper industry has evolved from one dominated by a small number of private firms to one in which much of the world's production is controlled by national governments. Decolonialization, nationalism, and Third World development programs have all contributed to the expansion of capacity in developing countries.

The domestic copper industry operates with two distinct disadvantages: low ore grades and high labor costs. In addition, domestic mines operate under stringent environmental regulations that incur substantial costs that are not borne by mines in most other countries. Despite these disadvantages the domestic industry has been able to maintain a significant share of the world copper market. This is the result of two factors: the economics of surface mining and a large base of existing copper smelters and refineries. U.S. copper production is based to a large degree on low-grade copper porphyry deposits. Domestic deposits are made competitive through the use of large-scale open pit mines, combined with technology that can be used near the mine to concentrate the copper-bearing minerals into a concentrate averaging above 30 percent copper. This copper concentrate can be transported economically to smelters located farther from the mine and then to refineries for purification and sale. Finally, the markets are nearby via efficient distribution systems.

Increased energy costs during the 1970s raised the cost of smelting and refining copper. New environmental regulations also increased operating costs, particularly at the smelting stage. Over the decade from 1975 to 1985 these cost increases led to the decline of copper capacity in older plants, but this was partially offset by the introduction of solvent extraction/electrowinning (SX/EW) technology as an alternative to the smelting process (see Figure 2-2) for suitable ores. This technology proved invaluable to the competitiveness of domestic copper producers. As a result of the closing of the most costly facilities and deposits and the introduction of new processing facilities based on SX/EW technology, the copper industry was restructured into one that could compete in the world market.

Lead

The domestic lead industry is the largest producer in the world, accounting for 11 percent of the world's mine production. Lead is generally mined

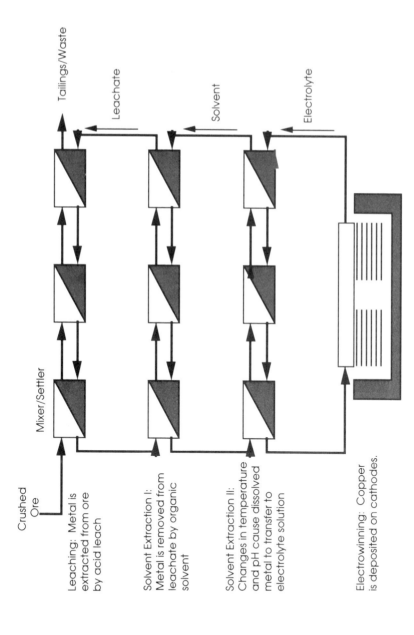

FIGURE 2-2 Solvent extraction/electrowinning technology.

Solvent Extraction/Electrowinning Plant at San Manuel Mine, Arizona. (Courtesy Magma Copper Company.)

using underground mining methods. Crushed ore from the mine is hauled to mills in preparation for smelting and refining. Lead coproducts include zinc, which is usually recovered during the milling stage, and silver and copper, both of which may be by-products of the refining process.

The discovery and development of significant new lead deposits in Missouri strengthened the industry during the 1960s and 1970s. This region now accounts for over 90 percent of U.S. production. Although the Missouri ores are relatively low in lead content, they are easily amenable to mechanized mining, beneficiation, and smelting. As a result, energy and labor costs in the domestic lead industry can be as low per pound of lead as they are in other producing countries; the relative simplicity of mining, processing, and smelting provides an advantage to offset the higher grade but mineralogically more complex ores of foreign producers. Thus, the industry can compete with foreign producers, at least in the domestic market where foreign producers must also face shipping costs.

Most foreign lead production is tightly integrated with the production of other metals. Thus, foreign lead production can be affected by changes in demand for other metals, particularly silver and zinc. Domestic producers, with less by-product production, are less sensitive to demand variations in other metals. At times this may work to the competitive advantage of the domestic industry, while at other times it may hurt profitability.

The lead industry must comply with environmental and safety standards, both in the mining and processing of ore and in the disposal of tailings and waste products. Health and environmental regulations have been a burden to the lead industry, although less than to the copper industry, which required major investments in new smelters. Even so, regulation of the lead industry has added some costs, and when, as now, standards are set more strictly in the United States than in foreign locations, they reduce the competitiveness of the domestic industry relative to foreign producers. The industry must identify and apply cost-effective means of complying with these standards in order to avoid losing a competitive edge to other producing countries that do not apply such standards. At the same time, capital costs of new smelting methods, coupled with problems in plants presently implementing these technologies, have deterred their introduction in the United States.

Zinc

Zinc is produced both by itself and as a coproduct of lead production. Underground mining is used in all but a few foreign deposits using traditional mining technologies and various techniques for separating zinc minerals from gangue. Zinc metal is obtained from the concentrated ore by chemical or pyrometallurgical means, then refined and cast into slabs or processed into sheet, strip, or other forms for commercial sale.

The domestic zinc industry has two disadvantages relative to foreign producers. The first is a low ore grade—U.S. ores average less than half the zinc content of foreign ores. The second factor is the low content of by- and coproduct metals. In U.S. deposits zinc appears as the primary constituent, whereas in other countries it is often part of a complex ore containing significant amounts of lead and precious metals.

Domestic zinc production has remained competitive due to high domestic labor productivity and capital facilities already in place. The competitiveness of domestic zinc production would be greatly enhanced by the exploitation of higher-grade deposits. Deposits with high contents of zinc and other metals, like the Red Dog deposit in Alaska, could significantly change the apparent competitive status of the domestic zinc mining industry, even though the concentrates may go to foreign smelters.

TRENDS IN METALS DEMAND

Current Status of Materials Demand

Near-term projections of demand for metals can be derived from current demand patterns and from projections for growth of major metal-consuming industries. Such projections must be tempered by experience and a knowledge of underlying trends in substitution, changing intensity of use, and other relevant factors. Since it takes several years for major changes in these factors to permeate industry, this methodology can provide usable estimates for the 5- to 10-year time frame. In the longer term the demand for metals will also reflect changes in system design, availability of new materials and processes, and other factors that affect the intensity of use of

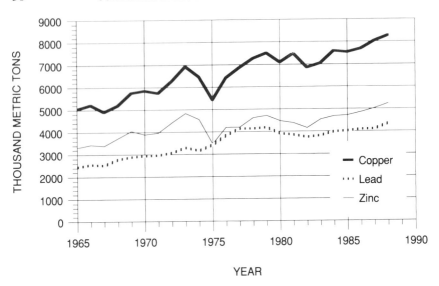

FIGURE 2-3 Base metal consumption, 1965-1988 (world, excluding Eastern European socialist countries). Source: Metallgesellschaft, A.G. Metal Statistics.

metals in manufacturing. It will also reflect some of the profound political changes now sweeping the globe.

Metal demand is driven by the requirements of the economy's manufacturing sectors (e.g., automobiles, aviation, and construction). It is affected by substitution, both by alternative metals and alloys and by nonmetallic materials (e.g., plastics and composites). Demand is also affected by conservation efforts, both intentional (as with recycling of scrap produced in the manufacturing process) and side effects (as in the use of near-net-shape forging and powder metallurgy).

Figure 2-3 illustrates patterns in base metal consumption over the past 25 years for the Western industrialized countries. The period of stagnation from the mid-1970s to the mid-1980s included two recessions, the end of the Vietnam War, two major increases in energy costs, and a gradual shift in the economies of developed countries from manufacturing to services. In the past few years, however, metals consumption has begun to increase more rapidly. This increased demand, combined with reduced capacity, has resulted in higher metal prices, which have returned the minerals and metals industry to profitability

Near-Term Trends in Materials Consumption

Future demand for metals will be strongly affected by the growth of the economy as a whole. As shown in Figure 2-4, developing countries are

projected to have the greatest rate of increase in the growth of their economies. This growth will also have an effect on the distribution of the growth
of metals markets in the future.

Demand is also affected by the intensity of use (I/U) of a metal in a
society's economy. I/U is measured as the amount of material consumed
(usually) on a weight basis divided by the gross national product (GNP). I/
U use is dynamic, reflecting changes in the technologies used by the manufacturing
sector and changes in the mix of agricultural, manufacturing, and service
industries in the overall economy. In general, the I/U of metals rises as an
economy develops. Once the industrial infrastructure is complete, however,
the growth of I/U will slow, with the pattern for individual metals reflecting
the particular mix of industries in the national economy. In a mature economy,
growth shifts to the service industries, reducing the relative contribution of
manufacturing and materials to GNP and causing a decline in the I/U of
metals.

Trends in Industry Use of Materials

Domestic demand for metals can be estimated in terms of the cumulative
demand across the major sectors of the economy. This approach provides

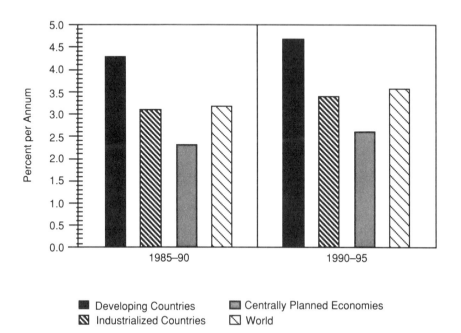

FIGURE 2-4 Projected GNP growth rates, 1985-1995. Source: World Bank.

an understanding about the potential for demand changes in the future. The present domestic consumption by industry sector of aluminum, copper, iron and steel, lead, and zinc is shown in Figure 2-5.

Automotive Industry. The automotive industry is a major consumer of metals and other materials, but the roles of specific materials are changing. Steel remains the principal material for the chassis, but composite materials and molded plastics have captured significant portions of the body and trim. Small parts and fittings that were once made of die-cast zinc are now generally made from plastic. Not all changes have led to reductions in metal use, however. Radiators, which once were copper, are now made of aluminum, and concern about rust and corrosion has led to increases in zinc coatings, virtually offsetting the decrease of zinc use due to reduced use of die castings. The changing role of materials in the auto industry is shown in Figure 2-6.

Materials selection for the automobile remains quite competitive. The development of new steel alloys, with properties tailored to the needs of the automotive industry, has helped the steel industry retain this market despite competition from nonmetallic materials. The copper industry also is striving to develop manufacturing processes that will provide performance and economic advantages over current aluminum designs of automobile radiators. The future demand for metals by the automotive industry will continue to reflect the traditional criteria of performance, cost, and reliability. How-

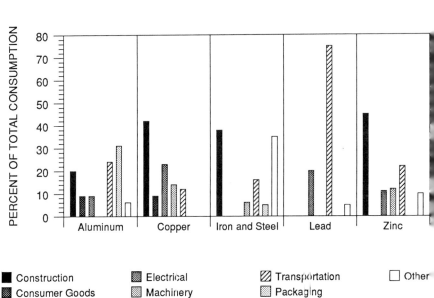

Source: Data from Bureau of Mines

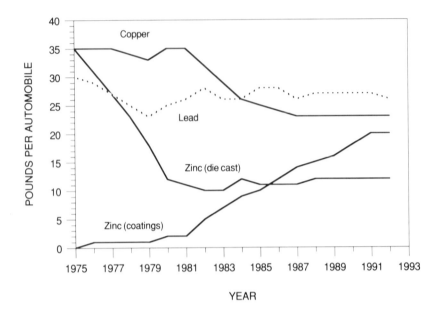

FIGURE 2-6 Automotive materials usage (base metals). Source: Ford Motor Company.

ever, increasing national concern about environmental quality and energy conservation is also likely to increase emphasis on fuel economy, emission control, and potential recycling of materials from obsolete automobiles, with possible implications for the selection of materials in the cars of the future.

Aviation Industry. Selection of materials for use in aircraft structural components also involves the traditional factors of cost, performance, weight, reliability, and fabricability. Different applications may vary in the emphasis they place on particular factors—military aircraft, for example, often accept increased cost in order to achieve improved performance—but weight and reliability are common concerns. Other goals pursued through materials selection include the following:

Fuel savings. In large transports the use of lighter materials could produce a savings of 15 to 20 gallons of fuel per year for each pound of weight reduction.

Reliability and durability. Specifications for the redesign of the A6 Intruder wing using composite materials call for a service life of 8,000 hours, compared with 2,000 hours for the current aluminum wing.

Aluminum has replaced most copper radiators and is used extensively in the automotive industry. Pictured is an aluminum radiator produced by Ford Motor Company. (Courtesy Ford Motor Company Research Staff.)

Light weight and high payload. The low weight of the V22 Osprey tilt-rotor vertical take off and landing (VTOL) is achieved in part through the use of a composite airframe, the first aircraft so designed.

Aluminum remains the dominant structural material for aircraft, but strong and lightweight composite materials developed in the 1960s have potential economic and performance advantages. As fabrication technology improved during the 1970s, these potential gains were exploited by designers of military aircraft. The experience gained in high-performance military applications is now leading to increased use of composites in commercial applications.

At the same time, however, the demand for higher performance has led to significant advances in metals and metal processing technologies to meet the needs of the air craft industry. These advances have come through three mechanisms: new alloys, alloy processing based on powders rather than melts, and precision casting and forging of large complicated parts. New alloys generally provide incremental improvements in materials properties and allow the continued use of existing fabrication processes. More revolutionary changes are possible as a result of new alloy production processes based on powder metallurgy. By creating alloys from powders rather than from molten solutions, this technique can create components and systems with desirable properties that would be impossible to produce by conventional metallurgy. Advances in fabrication processes have also improved the competitive situation of alloys by (1) reducing the fraction of metal lost to scrap, (2) eliminating one or more steps in the fabrication and assembly process, and (3) improving the quality and reliability of finished parts. The lower cost of casting and forging large complex shapes in single stages will continue to give an advantage to metals for complex shapes that must be mass produced, at least until performance requirements necessitate the use of special coatings or anisotropic materials, such as particulate-reinforced aluminums.

Titanium metal matrix composite reinforced with continuous silicon carbide fibers. This extruded I-beam structure was fabricated by North American Aviation, Rockwell International Corporation. Scale shown is in inches. (Courtesy Rockwell International Corporation.)

Building and Construction Industry. Building and construction account for 50 percent of zinc metal consumption, 42 percent of copper, and 35 percent of iron and steel but less than 25 percent of lead and only a small percentage of aluminum. Demand in this sector could change in the future due to three factors: changes in the construction rate, changes in the materials used, and/or changes in the mix of structures and facilities constructed.

One major factor affecting future consumption in this sector is the impending need to rebuild much of the domestic transportation and utility infrastructure. A commitment to rebuild, rather than to repair and maintain, could result in a sharp increase in the consumption of most metals: steel in bridges, railroads, building structures, and reinforcing rod; copper in electric wiring and plumbing; zinc in plumbing and as a coating for steel; lead in wire sheathing, noise reduction, and additives in asphalt; and aluminum in road signs and roadside railings.

Chemical Industry. The chemical industry is a heavy user of metals in structural applications as well as in piping, pressure vessels, and other chemical processing equipment. Stainless and alloy steels and surface-treated steels, brass, and bronze are all used in the production of chemicals. Similar materials are also required in large-scale production of biomaterials. In the future, hazardous waste treatment facilities will be a growing consumer of metals.

Electronics Industry. Modern electronic transmission and storage systems utilize a number of metals that are obtained as coproducts of the minerals and metals industry (see Table 2-2). Demand for these metals will continue to increase with the growth in consumption of semiconductors and electro-optical devices. Demand will vary over time as specific end users adopt new technologies—for example, the telephone system shifting from copper wire (for the transmission of electric signals) to glass fiber (for the transmission of light).

Magnetic materials are used in the long-term storage of information, including both consumer goods (audio and video recording tape) and computer storage devices (data tape and magnetic storage disks). For example, magnetic coatings containing 80 to 85 percent cobalt greatly increase storage density. Demand for these materials will continue to increase as new computers are designed with tolerances that can take advantage of this increased capacity. Long-term demand is less clear, particularly as optical storage systems begin to compete with magnetic media in computer workstations. The electro-optical systems now entering the market use a laser to heat a spot on a thin film of rare earth metal to a point where it can switch its polarity. This results in a system with extremely high information density: a single optoelectronic storage disk, for example, can hold approximately

TABLE 2-2 Metals in Electronic Applications

Copper	Electrical wiring
Cobalt	Magnetic data-storage devices
Platinum group metals (platinum, palladium, rhodium, ruthenium, iridium, osmium)	Electrical contacts, multilayer capacitors, conductive and resistive films, crucibles for production of electronic materials and devices, dental materials
Gold	Electroplating and wiring in integrated circuits and electronic devices
Silver	Wiring and capacitors
Silicon	Semiconductor devices and photovoltaic cells
Cadmium	Batteries
Gallium	Gallium-arsenide electro-optical devices, integrated circuits, and possibly solar energy conversion devices
Germanium	Infrared optical devices, fiber optics, windows for transmission of infrared light
Mercury	Batteries
Selenium	Photoreceptors in electrophotographic copiers
Tellurium	Infrared sensing materials (mercury-cadmium-tellurium compounds), photocopiers
Tantalum	Capacitors
Indium	High-performance solder, solar cells, and optical coatings

250 megabytes of data, compared with 20 to 30 megabytes in a similar size of hard disk unit. Growing demand for these high-capacity storage systems will continue to drive demand for advanced magnetic materials, but these materials will be applied in extremely small amounts per unit.

Energy Industry. The energy industry is another major consumer of metals. Aluminum and copper are the primary conductors of electricity. Steel is required for construction of power plants, and zinc is used to protect the surface of steel from corrosion. Demand for metals in the future depends in part on the future mix of technologies used to produce energy. If central fossil fuel plants are constructed, for example, demand will continue to be high for structural steel, zinc coatings, and aluminum and copper wire. If power-leveling systems are introduced on a large scale, however, requirements for structural steel may decline while other metals, particularly lead, zinc, or platinum, may rise in demand for their use in power-storage systems. Small solar energy facilities for generating electricity or heating water could reduce the need for long-distance transportation of electricity, thereby reducing demand for aluminum and copper wire.

Telecommunications Industry. Copper was the principal medium for transmitting signals from the development of the telegraph until the introduction of microwave systems and the communications satellite, and even then it continued to be essential in local systems and trunk lines. This use will decline with the growing use of fiber optic communication networks. Already in use for inter-city communication, fiber optic lines have been installed for trans-Atlantic communication and in the future may reach directly to local business and residential customers. However, the potential impact of the substitution of fiber optic materials is limited to the fraction of copper demand for telecommunications wiring, which is about 12 to 15 percent of total demand for copper. Even if fiber optic systems captured about 40 percent of this market by 1992, it would represent only 5 to 6 percent of total copper demand.

COMPETITIVENESS OF THE U.S. INDUSTRY

Competitiveness is frequently cited as a goal for U.S. industries in the world economy, but the concept of competitiveness is usually left undefined, both in general terms and with specific reference to individual industries. The committee's focus here is primarily on the competitiveness of the domestic minerals and metals industry vis-à-vis foreign industries and only secondarily on its competitiveness with respect to new materials and technologies. It is difficult to accurately assess the competitiveness of the U.S. minerals and metals industry as a whole. However, data on U.S. market share and net imports and exports provide a gauge of the revealed comparative advantage held by segments of the industry. (Revealed or apparent advantage refers to a company's or an industry's share of world production; real or actual advantage refers to relative costs of production.)

Shifts in U.S. Competitiveness

General Trends

One measure of competitiveness is the share of a market held by a firm or industry and whether that share is increasing or decreasing (see Box). Figure 2-7 presents the U.S. market share of world mine production in 1989, including the five industries specifically examined in this study. Note that the U.S. share exceeds 10 percent for only 6 of the 15 items. Table 2-3 shows that U.S. market share for four major commodity metals was lower in 1988 than it was in 1975 and lower than it was in 1980 in all but copper. This illustrates the point made earlier, that industries may cut costs and be profitable but still lose market share.

Figure 2-8 shows the net reliance on imports to satisfy U.S. demand for

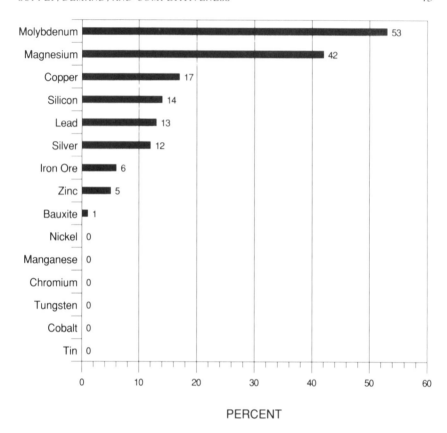

PERCENT

FIGURE 2-7 U.S. market share of world mine production, 1989. Source: Bureau of Mines.

various minerals and metals in 1989. The change in net import reliance across several years for selected minerals and metals is shown in Table 2-4. Overall the decline in the value of the dollar and other factors have brought the minerals trade deficit down to a level of $10 billion in 1989, compared with $13 billion in 1987 and $15 billion in 1986. About half of the current deficit is attributable to net imports of iron and steel. The domestic industry is a net exporter of only five commodity metals: gold, magnesium, molybdenum, metal scrap, and recently aluminum.

Competitiveness by Sector

The U.S. metals industry (with one or two relatively minor exceptions) is no longer the dominant player in the world market. This is probably a

MATERIALS COMPETITION IN THE MANUFACTURING SECTOR

The design engineer in the manufacturing industries must consider a new material—and its associated fabrication process—in the context of replacing a material/process combination that is already in production for a given component. In some cases a totally new part is designed or an existing part is extensively redesigned to take advantage of the high-performance properties of the new material and its process. In other cases several existing parts may be combined into a single integrated component that can be produced with greater reliability or at lower cost.

The factors that affect materials selection decisions are key to understanding the potential for changes in the intensity of use of specific metals in the manufacturing industries. To make the discussion concrete, choices in the automotive sector are discussed. Similar processes are generally followed in other industries.

As a new model of automobile is designed or as innovations are introduced, the designer may consider using a new material if it offers some benefit, such as

- higher performance (e.g., improved fuel economy and/or reduced engine noise and vibration);
- lower cost (e.g., less costly materials, less costly processing, lower tooling costs, lower warranty costs, etc.);
- weight savings; and
- styling (exterior and interior) flexibility.

The designer must be assured that the new material will provide equal or better functional performance (e.g., strength, stiffness, crash durability) or reduced material or production cost relative to conventional materials and processes. This may be accomplished through prototype testing, computer simulation, or other means of evaluation. If the testing supports the potential benefits of the alternative material, further studies will be undertaken.

While performance, shape and packaging feasibility issues are being resolved, the designer also works with the manufacturing engineer to determine the manufacturing feasibility of the part. In the past, designers often handed off the component design to the manufacturing engineers at the completion of the design process. As a result, manufacturing issues were not resolved until late in the product development process. Today, however, designers work closely with manufacturing engineers to resolve manufacturing issues during the early design stage.

Often the first manufacturing consideration is whether the part can be made utilizing the selected processing method. For example, high-strength steels generally cannot be stamped with the same die shape used for mild steel. Even with die modifications it may not be possible to form some complex shapes. These issues must be resolved in the prototype trials, or alternative fabrication processes must be selected.

Once manufacturing feasiblity is established in the prototype stage, a decision has to be made as to whether the manufacturing system should be scaled up to the pilot stage. This is done to gain confidence that the parts can be made with very low variability at high production volumes. Since this is a critical step as well as an expensive one, only a few projects are selected for this stage. Pilot demonstrations are necessary in order to identify problems that could arise in a full-scale production plant.

While functional performance and manufacturing feasibility are being assessed, the costs associated with producing the new material/process combination are being evaluated. As confidence in manufacturing grows, the cost estimates become more accurate.

It is important to note that the materials cost is only one factor to be considered. One must also take into account all of the other costs involved in the component subsystem and ultimately in the total vehicle system.

Even if the cost of an individual component made from an alternative material is higher than the part currently in use, it may be used under certain conditions:

• if it contributes to a new product feature, so that it can be priced to retain or improve economic profit;
• if it improves reliability, contributing to a favorable warranty impact;
• if it is required to meet government regulations and the additional costs offset the costs elsewhere in the product; or
• if it is required to meet competition, and the increase in variable costs could be offset either in the same subsystem or elsewhere in the vehicle.

Another important factor is the supplier infrastructure. Some industries purchase about 50 percent of the materials for use in their manufactured products either in the form of semifinished products or components and subsystems. Since the automobile manufacturer is virtually dependent on its suppliers for the ultimate quality of the products, it will prefer to use suppliers with an established record of producing high-quality materials and parts at high production volume.

In introducing a new materials technology, it is quite possible that there is no current established supplier, either external or internal, willing to take the risk of investing in the new technology. Or a firm outside the traditional supplier industry may promise to supply the new technology but lack a track record of supplying high quality at high production volumes. There is a reluctance on the part of many purchasing organizations to make agreements with such firms. In other cases a start-up firm that has no established materials processing capability—only a prototyping capability—may be the potential supplier. This is the most difficult situation of all, since it entails the greatest combination of uncertainties.

Based on the above analysis, the following conclusions are drawn regarding changes in materials use in the automobile industry:

• Radical changes in materials and manufacturing technology are unlikely due to the huge investment in existing materials and processes and the requirement that investment in new technology be profitable in the fairly near term.
• New materials will be introduced in incremental fashion, building on existing high-volume production processes that have either been developed internally, by current suppliers, or by other industries.
• Once a foothold has been established in one or two parts, diffusion occurs in a part-by-part manner, as the new infrastructure builds.

While these conclusions are derived from the automobile industry, they are based on principles common to all manufacturing industries. As such, they provide a guide for evaluating the rate of change of metals use in the manufacturing sector as a whole.

TABLE 2-3 United States and World Production[a] of Selected Metals, 1975–1989 (thousand metric tons, except as noted)

	1975	1980	1983	1988	1989
Copper					
United States	1,282	1,181	1,038	1,420	1,500
World[b]	6,962	7,630	8,044	8,453	8,830
U.S. share of					
world production (%)	18.4	15.5	12.9	16.8	17.0
Iron Ore[c]					
United States	78.9	69.6	37.6	57.5	58.7
World[b]	877.6	873.6	729.6	916.0	943.1
U.S. share of					
world production (%)	9.0	8.0	5.1	6.3	6.2
Lead					
United States	564	551	466	394	450
World[b]	3,438	3,520	3,367	3,420	3,450
U.S. share of					
world production (%)	16.4	15.7	13.8	11.5	13.0
Zinc					
United States	426	317	275	256	345
World[b]	5,562	5,745	6,246	6,977	7,040
U.S. share of					
world production (%)	7.7	5.5	4.4	3.7	4.9

[a]Mine production.
[b]Inclusive of United States.
[c]Million long tons of ore.
SOURCE: Bureau of Mines, Mineral Commodity Summaries (various years).

permanent change of status. Most of the metals subindustries are still attracting investment to existing facilities, but they are finding fewer and fewer opportunities for new "greenfield" developments. The only clear exceptions appear to be gold and silver and, on a much smaller scale, the platinum group metals. The U.S. share of world gold production rose from 7 percent in 1986 to nearly 13 percent in 1988. The domestic share of world silver production (mostly from coproduct mines) increased from 8 percent to 12 percent in the same 3-year period.

The domestic aluminum industry has adjusted to its changing economic circumstances sufficiently well that its competitive decline is now only gradual. Overall domestic capacity, which had declined steadily from 1983 to 1987, stabilized in 1988 when primary aluminum metal output rose by 17 percent, allowing exports to increase in 1989. The wrought aluminum sector should remain quite competitive; a start has been made on diversification and exploration of new materials and products.

Copper gained only moderately in comparison to other national industries—a 1 percent gain in market share during 1988, with no further gain in 1989. With low inventories, lower labor costs, and continued productivity improvements and restructuring, the U.S. copper industry is now somewhere in the middle of the competitiveness range internationally. The long-term outlook is for increasing materials substitution as well as increasingly strong competition from foreign producers, who are expanding aggressively and cutting costs. When demand turns downward, there may be a further shakeout of producers.

Table 2-3 shows that the domestic lead industry lost substantial portions of its market share during the 1980s. Domestic lead is in a period of transition, with recycling of scrap (mostly from car batteries) edging out primary refining of mine output. At the same time, world mine production is increasing, and while domestic lead is produced from essentially monometallic mines, much of the world obtains lead as a coproduct. Environmental concerns also affect the lead industry. For both lead and zinc the outlook

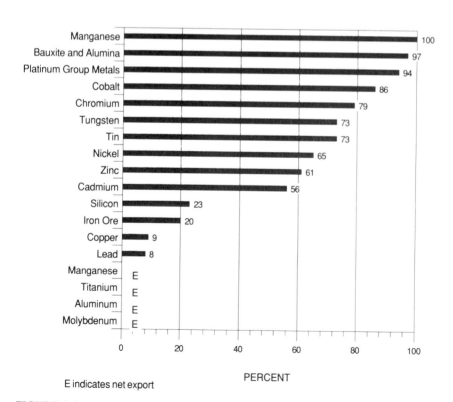

E indicates net export

PERCENT

FIGURE 2-8 Net import reliance for selected minerals and metals, 1989. Source: Bureau of Mines.

TABLE 2-4 Change in U.S. Net Import Reliance for Selected Minerals and Metals as a Percentage of Consumption, 1983–1989

	1983	1984	1985	1986	1987	1988	1989
Aluminum	17	7	16	26	23	7	E
Bauxite	96	96	96	96	96	97	97
Chromium	76	80	75	79	76	77	79
Cobalt	95	95	94	85	86	86	86
Copper	19	23	28	27	26	13	9
Iron ore	37	19	21	33	22	18	20
Iron and steel	16	23	22	21	19	17	13
Lead	20	20	12	20	17	13	8
Magnesium	E	E	E	E	E	E	E
Manganese	99	98	100	100	100	100	100
Molybdenum	7	E	E	E	E	E	E
Nickel	75	69	71	73	75	68	65
Platinum Group Metals	89	89	92	90	94	95	94
Silicon	31	18	25	36	33	29	23
Tin	73	74	72	74	74	78	73
Tungsten	52	70	68	70	79	76	73
Zinc	65	68	70	73	71	69	61

Notes: Net import reliance = imports − exports + adjustments for government and industry stock changes. Apparent consumption = U.S. primary and secondary production + net import reliance. E = net exporter.
SOURCE: Bureau of Mines, Mineral Commodity Summaries, 1990.

for future competitiveness is clouded by vulnerability to substitution by other materials and by higher-grade mixed deposits in other countries.

Despite moderate increases in production and profits, there has been only slight expansion or even contraction of the existing capacity of the U.S. iron and steel industry's large, highly integrated facilities. A positive development has appeared in the form of "mini-mills" or "market mills," which serve a selected geographic area by melting 100 percent scrap and continuously casting billets to be made into merchant shapes. They have captured a large share of the market for these less expensive materials from the integrated mills and now have plans to move into the more technologically demanding sheet market, an experiment that is being watched with interest. Meanwhile foreign competitors could further erode the integrated mills' market share in the future.

In 1986 the Congressional Research Service noted "a gradual deterioration of competitiveness mineral-by-mineral." This does indeed appear to be taking place, with uneven patterns of decline and resiliency across the subindustries. Despite the recent revival in prices, production, and profits in many subindustries, U.S. competitiveness in the minerals and metals industry appears to be continuing the pattern of gradual decline that has held since World War II.

Comparative Advantages and Disadvantages of the U.S. Industry

Previous sections of this chapter have noted most of the reasons for the competitive status of the U.S. industry and its subindustries—whether growing, holding steady, or declining. No single reason explains their current competitive situations, even for those that are declining. However, some factors are certainly more important and broader in their impact.

Table 2-5 summarizes the factors responsible for the current state of the U.S. mining and metals industry. Factors are not listed strictly in order of importance, although in general the more significant ones do appear earlier. In all it is obvious that the list of disadvantages is far more extensive than the list of advantages enjoyed by the industry. The comparative disadvantages are both real and revealed—that is, some have a direct impact on production costs at the mine or refinery, while others "tilt the playing field" against the domestic producers. Of the advantages, the first three are real advantages, while the other three are a function of government policies at home and abroad.

These factors have an immediate day-to-day impact on the competitiveness of the U.S. mining and minerals industry, but the industry also faces a number of longer-term background problems that are undermining its health and overall ability to compete. One of the most significant of these is the lack of an adequate science base to support mining and processing technology development. It is not that the United States lags other nations in the relevant science and technology, but rather that the domestic industry must rely more heavily on technology to maintain its competitiveness. The problem is one of insufficiently imaginative research, exacerbated by poor communication between academic researchers and the engineers who deal with the real technical problems in the industry. (See Chapter 4 for a further discussion of institutional roles in mining research and technology transfer.)

Financial factors present another difficulty for the U.S. industry. Companies in sectors other than precious metals have difficulty finding capital. This difficulty derives from the industry's poor investment image coupled with the prevailing emphasis by investors on short-term earnings.

Technology and U.S. Comparative Advantage

Chapter 3 of this report addresses the role of science and technology in the competitiveness of the minerals and metals industry. Nevertheless, several points are relevant to this discussion of comparative advantages and

TABLE 2-5 Factors Affecting the Competitiveness of the U.S. Minerals and Metals Industry

The domestic minerals and metals industry has had to cope with a number of factors that work to its *disadvantage* relative to foreign producers and processors. Among these are:

- Decline in ore grades in domestic deposits, relative to the high-quality ores being found in many developing countries.
- Increasing development of facilities for downstream processing by foreign producers, resulting in overcapacity and overproduction.
- Rapidity of international development and transfer of technology at moderate cost, minimizing the comparative advantage in technology traditionally enjoyed by U.S. producers.
- Comparative disadvantage in labor costs, relative to the lower wage rates prevailing in nearly all other producer countries. (Depending on the country, this differential has shrunk and even disappeared with the recent drop in the value of the dollar; indeed, the labor cost differential has shrunk steadily for decades.)
- Relative decline in the size of the U.S. domestic market in comparison to the world market.
- Fluctuations in exchange rates, which in the past have tended to favor imports rather than exports of U.S. minerals.
- Restricted access for some U.S. exports in some international markets.
- Ready availability of capital from international lending organizations for foreign mining and processing operations. (Lending institutions have tightened criteria for financing resource development projects, so this factor will be less important in the future.)
- Readiness of some foreign governments to continue production at levels not supported by the market in order to maintain jobs and income stream (i.e., production objectives not tied to price), whereas the U.S. government relies primarily on free markets.
- Presence of substantial coproducts (or by-products) in many foreign ore bodies, yielding multiple income streams.
- Shift toward incentives for short-term financial objectives and planning horizons of U.S. corporate management, along with injurious financial manipulation.
- Rising cost of energy relative to that of many other countries (especially in the case of the aluminum industry).
- Cost burden of compliance with environmental, land use, and safety regulations that are more stringent than those borne by foreign producers.
- A more pronounced shift toward alternative materials and less metal-intensive products in the domestic economy than in other markets.
- Loss of public support and confidence (poor image).
- Changes in ownership of U.S. companies and erratic management performance, at least in the recent past.

The following factors operate to the *advantage* of U.S. producers, relative to those of most foreign countries:

- High productivity of the domestic work force (better use of technology is a factor here, as are work rules that permit new flexibilities and multifunctional workers).
- Faster access to new technologies.
- Lower transportation costs in serving most of the large U.S. market.
- Less interference by the government.
- Lower net tax burden (some foreign governments require substantial direct payments—copper, lead, and zinc are industries in which the United States has a significantly smaller tax burden).
- Market-determined input prices (i.e., some foreign industries pay arbitrary prices for raw materials).

---

disadvantages. Technology can contribute to a competitive advantage in three ways. The first is through exclusive access to a technology that increases the productivity of a mine or improves the quality of the product. Given the speed with which information travels between firms and countries, this advantage is temporary, but the first firm or country to implement a valuable technology may acquire a comparative advantage for several years before it spreads to others in the industry. New technologies have their greatest impact when they can be integrated into the design of a new facility, however, and most new mines and processing plants are being built overseas.

The second way in which technology can contribute to a comparative advantage is when it addresses conditions or circumstances unique to a firm or country. Factors that affect U.S. industry to a greater degree than other countries include high labor costs, low ore grades, and more stringent environmental regulation. These factors therefore provide targets of opportunity for research and development (R&D) that will provide a comparative advantage for domestic operations. Technologies to concentrate metal from low-grade ores, to increase labor productivity, and to reduce the cost of meeting environmental standards all would contribute more extensively to U.S. firms than to foreign producers. Nevertheless, it may be somewhat simplistic to believe that more R&D alone is the solution to the difficulties of the domestic mining and minerals industry.

The third way in which technology may affect competitiveness is by allowing metal producers to adapt to changing consumer demand by producing metals that meet new quality and performance needs. Competition between materials becomes most intense when systems undergo extensive redesign, but such opportunities are not frequent; the automotive design cycle is about

10 years in duration (component changes alone may take 3 or more years to implement), and in aviation the design cycle is at least that long, especially for commercial aircraft. Domestic metal producers may earn a comparative advantage relative to both foreign metal producers and producers of nonmetallic materials by collaborating with designers and fabricators in the development of the next generation of manufactured products. In aviation, for example, aluminum producers devote funds and personnel to efforts to develop alloys and metal processing techniques that meet the requirements of the next generation of aircraft.

Data Analysis for Materials Planning

Clearly, changes in technology will produce changes in the demand for raw materials and for intermediate products, including alloys, metal powders, and other metal products. Companies that wish to become or remain competitive will need to anticipate future demand changes in order to respond quickly when those changes occur. While there is no way for them to accurately predict the future, it is feasible to project the implications of technological changes on materials demand and to then base R&D, exploration, and investment decisions on assessments of the likelihood of those changes actually being implemented. This type of analysis is referred to as indicative planning.

Data for indicative planning can be organized into input-output tables that expose overall patterns of demand for primary materials and how they change as consumer purchases of manufactured products go up and down. Input-output models can also be used to evaluate the impact of technological changes on demand for raw and semiprocessed materials. Such projections would be of substantial importance for assessing the capability of the domestic economy to meet the requirements of public projects ranging from military and defense programs to rebuilding the domestic transportation infrastructure.

The ability to conduct this type of analysis rests on the availability of current and reliable data about the manufacturing economy. Much of the relevant data are obtained by the Bureau of the Census through the Census of Manufacturers. Other relevant data have been generated by outside consulting firms, such as Battelle Columbus Laboratories and SRI International, and by university research projects and federal laboratories. The Bureau of Mines, working with the Bureau of the Census and with public and private research organizations, should evaluate the need of a consolidated, accessible database for purposes of indicative planning.

Government support for materials science should recognize that traditional metal alloys will remain contenders for use in the manufacturing and infrastructure sectors. Advances in materials science and engineering can contribute both to the performance and the competitiveness of metals and metal products. Support for basic research should not be cut in order to transfer funds to support research in alternative materials. Such research may be deserving of support on its own merits in addition to, but not in place of, support for minerals and metals research and the development of improved manufacturing technology.

3
Role of Science and Technology in Minerals and Metals Competitiveness Issues

To be truly competitive in the nonrenewable resource sector, a firm or industry must locate new economic raw material sources and also maintain, update, and replace its production and processing facilities as costs, technologies, and regulatory requirements change. In the minerals and metals industry in particular, exploration accomplishes the former function, while mining and process research and development (R&D) fulfill the latter. In financially difficult times these functions require corporate commitment, maintenance of an effective infrastructure, and the availability of money on a sustained basis.

A technology-based competitive strategy cannot be developed without a long-term commitment of intellectual and financial resources. Creative interdisciplinary thinking and experimentation by well-trained scientists and engineers, using modern equipment in well-equipped laboratories and pilot-plant facilities, can lead to both evolutionary and revolutionary technologies. If companies, universities, and governmental organizations commit to this strategy over the long term by supporting research and implementing its most promising products, U.S. firms will be competitive producers of minerals and metals, adapting relatively easily to changing economic and environmental conditions and requirements.

Evolutionary developments incrementally improve the efficiency of an existing technology. For instance, a larger truck to haul larger loads is an evolutionary enhancement, since the principles of the truck remain unchanged. Revolutionary research transforms a system. The advent of in situ extraction is an example of a revolutionary advance, since it rendered many of the basic extraction techniques obsolete.

This chapter identifies the technological developments that will be required to strengthen the competitiveness of the U.S. minerals and metals industry. The commodities it examines are the base metals, iron and steel, aluminum, and the precious metals. Coal and the industrial minerals are also included, since the technologies serving them may also have applications to the minerals and metals considered in this report. The chapter is divided into the four components of the mining industry: exploration, mining, minerals processing, and metals extraction. Within each of these four sections the state-of-the-art techniques and the research efforts of the U.S. minerals and metals industry are reviewed. The research strategies (both evolutionary and revolutionary) with the greatest potential impact on the competitiveness of the U.S. minerals and metals industry are also identified.

BACKGROUND

Although mining's origins can be traced back through five or six millennia, its modern structure is about 200 years old. The explosive growth in mechanics during the nineteenth century greatly improved the primitive devices for size reduction and gravity concentration that had been in use for over 500 years. Dynamite, compressed-air-driven tools, and most of the crushing and grinding machinery in use today were all developed before 1900. Meanwhile, gravity concentration was vastly improved by the mechanization of older devices and the invention of shaking tables. By the end of the nineteenth century, gravity's preeminence was challenged first by magnetic and electrostatic methods for mineral separation and then by the development of flotation.

Goals for developing new technology in mineral processing were identified at least as early as 1866 (Huet, 1866):

> . . . to reduce the intervention of the worker by extension of mechanical treatment . . . to reduce [waste] . . . by continually improving equipment . . . and to replace the intelligent attention of the workers by mechanical precision . . .

More recently, Revnivtsev (1988) wrote:

> . . . although five years ago the use of the word revolution in mineral processing might have been questioned, today the word should be underlined; starting with comminution, this technology is facing the necessity of creating and implementing new principles of ore breakage on a large scale.

These forecasts have come not from the industry but from its service sector, the research and consulting development arm. Industry itself has been far less enthusiastic with respect to the introduction of new technology. As noted by the Office of Technology Assessment (OTA), there have been few revolutionary advances in mining technology since the 1950s:

> Witness a 1983 U.S. Bureau of Mines report on Technological Innovation in the Copper Industry . . . that had to stretch its time frame to the last 30 to 50 years to develop a list of innovations. Instead, incremental improvements in existing methods, and adaptations of other types of technology to mining (e.g., computers, conveyor systems) have gradually reduced costs and increased productivity (OTA, 1988, p. 119).

The conclusion to be drawn is that meaningful dialogue is often lacking between the engineers who operate mines and plants and those engaged in R&D, both in companies and in service organizations. In too many cases both the targets for innovation and the efforts to address them have been defined by the service sector; but the industry's resistance to adopting anything significantly new ranges from formidable to insurmountable. Few companies have taken positive roles in developing new technologies, and these have been primarily in extractive metallurgy, particularly in the development of new or substantially modified smelting or leaching processes. Much of this technology has come from abroad or was first tested by smaller domestic companies. Among the best-known examples are Outokumpu's and Inco's flash smelting, initially developed in the 1940s and 1950s and very slowly adopted by U.S. firms.

Some of the same companies that exhibit strong resistance to accepting new technology from the outside, however, are heavily involved in developing new technology internally when compelling needs are recognized by management or forced on it by new regulations. This contradictory attitude raises important questions about the conduct of mining and minerals R&D:

- What are the areas of major importance?
- What opportunities exist for incremental or evolutionary improvements in technology to contribute to competitiveness?
- What are the most promising areas for revolutionary improvements in technology for the mining and metals industry?

EXPLORATION TECHNOLOGIES

Exploration techniques are used to locate and evaluate minerals deposits for potential mining and metal extraction. U.S. mineral exploration has been largely commodity specific over the past 50 years. Certain materials have been in great demand during specific periods, as with the uranium "rush" of the 1950s and early 1970s and the porphyry copper boom of the 1960s. Although precious metals currently command the majority of exploration budgets, there is increasing activity in copper (particularly oxide copper), other base metals, strategic metals (e.g., the platinum group metals), rare earths, beryllium, germanium, gallium, manganese, and titanium.

Exploration Geology

Computers and selectively sensitive sensors have greatly affected exploration geology in recent years. Reconnaissance data can now be obtained through a personal computer using time-share services such as GEOREF to collect bibliographical references. The U.S. Geological Survey's Mineral Resources Data System and the Bureau of Mines' Mineral Availability System provide site-specific mineral deposits and occurrence data and site maps. Models have also become increasingly important to exploration; many are based on new information related to regional and plate tectonics. At least one computer program, Prospector, has incorporated such data and permits the user to identify a particular model for a region depending on the geological information input. The program's projection can be used to enhance and refine subsequent detailed explorations.

Mapping and Surveying

The basic data collection stage of exploration programs has been greatly enhanced in recent years by the increased availability of aerial and satellite photo coverage. Base maps can now be prepared quickly and cheaply. The availability of high-quality color and infrared photos are a great aid to geologic mapping and interpretation. At the engineering stage the current generation of electronic distance-measuring instruments has enhanced speed and accuracy in establishing benchmarks, triangulation stations, property boundaries, drill hole locations, geophysical stations, and other data for which accurate topographic control is required. Finally, a great deal of geographic and topographic data can be entered and retrieved from computer data bases. The various computer-aided drafting programs can readily produce maps and sections at any scale required and can be color coded as desired.

Geophysics

Geophysical activities and surveys have not advanced as rapidly in the past 10 years as previously. Magnetics, electromagnetics, induced polarization, and, to a lesser degree, gravity and seismic probes are still widely used, both ground based and airborne. Some variations are now also being exploited, such as gradiometry and controlled-source magnetotellurics. The most important results of recent research have been improvements in reliability and reductions in the weight of solid-state instrumentation. Ultrasensitive gravimeters, particularly gravity-time-variation detectors, offer a powerful new geophysical tool. From the standpoint of regional airborne studies, electronic positioning systems such as Ranger or Loran can provide positional data within 5 meters. The ability to record digital data allows further data manipulation, filtering, and enhancement for better interpretation.

One technique widely accepted in both the minerals and petroleum industries is bore-hole logging. Probes now available include acoustic velocity, natural gamma, self-potential, resistivity, caliper, fluid resistivity and high-resolution temperature, bore-hole azimuth and inclination, dip meter, gamma-gamma density, neutron, induced polarization, and spectral gamma. These sensors can be used alone or in various combinations. Many of these functions provide information useful in both mining and geotechnical engineering.

Geochemistry

The use of geochemistry as an exploration tool at both the regional and the site-specific scales has increased greatly over the past 20 years. A scientific basis for sampling has been developed to identify geologic anomalies despite errors in sampling and sample preparation. Some of the more exciting developments in geochemistry have been advances in the technology of sampling through the transported overburden. In addition to improved lightweight drills and augers, some new techniques require no physical penetration of the overburden. Biogeochemistry, in particular sampling of plants with deep root systems, has shown very encouraging results. A recently developed technique that is still largely experimental involves the detection and quantitative determination of specific bacteria that are known to have an affinity for certain metals. This technology may have widespread applications in the future. Another technique being researched and used to some extent is soil gas geochemistry as a means of locating minerals not visible on the surface without the expense and time required for drilling and testing core samples.

Analytical techniques have also improved in recent years, particularly in the field of trace element determination. Although a fire assay is still considered the final answer for precious metals, the accuracy and precision of atomic absorption analyses have been improved. Also, resonance-enhanced multiphoton ionization (REMPI) and laser-induced fluorescence have made element-specific trace analysis possible at far lower concentration levels. Techniques such as induction coupled plasma (ICP) provide multielement trace element data at a fraction of the cost of individual element analyses. Likewise, neutron activation analysis (NAA) shows great promise in high-precision multielement determinations. Portable field analyzers based on variations of x-ray fluorescence technology are becoming widely used, particularly in operating mines where element concentrations are in ore-grade ranges; these instruments are quite useful in rapid scanning of drill core, working faces, and outcrops.

Computer statistical and graphic techniques are widely used in the interpretation and presentation of survey results. Some of the more sophisti-cated multivariate statistical methods have proven successful in the detection of subtle anomalies, particularly in regional surveys. Computer surface modeling and geostatistics are widely used in early-stage interpretation and evalua-tion of deposits.

Drilling Technology

Core drilling is still widely used in mineral exploration, although rotary and percussion methods enjoy a high popularity, particularly in precious metals exploration. The improvements in core drilling in recent years have been in the areas of hydraulics, instrumentation, and mechanical systems. New bit designs and improved mud and chemical additives have helped improve core recovery. More attention has been given in recent years to sample collection and preparation. Numerous sample collection devices are now on the market that collect multiple representative samples of drill cut-tings or other crushed material. Directional control of small-diameter drill holes has also improved. In addition to the old photographic methods, gyroscopic and laser systems are available.

Directions for Future R&D

It is an adage within the minerals industry that discovering a good new deposit is better than trying to improve the yield from a poor one with the use of advanced mining and processing technologies. If it is assumed that undiscovered rich ore bodies are still extant within the United States, the evolutionary improvement of exploratory technologies could enhance the competitiveness of the U.S. minerals and metals industry by allowing the discovery of new viable deposits. Evolutionary improvements in exploratory technologies include

- spatial and spectral image resolution to penetrate foliage and surface cover;
- digital geophysical coverage of the United States magnetically, gravi-tationally, radiometrically, and spectrally to a scale of one-half mile;
- improved drilling/sampling techniques and analytical methods to increase basic geophysical knowledge; and
- deep drilling of epithermal zones (15,000 to 25,000 feet).

Improvements in data bases and increased availability of information would allow smaller aggressive companies to perform effective exploration without prohibitive expense. Another research advance that could revolutionize the industry would be a more complete general theory of ore genesis and deposition, which would not only improve the probability of discovering new deposits but also aid in the development of new mines and the selection of more efficient extraction methodologies.

MINING TECHNOLOGIES

Current Mining Technologies

Mining technologies are those required to expose and remove ores and minerals from their natural deposits. The development of current mining technologies reflects the following factors:

• Cost of labor (both wages and benefits) rose rapidly after World War II, forcing a relentless drive for higher productivity,
• Demand for mineral products and energy increased with World War II, the Korean War, and the postwar reconstruction in Europe and elsewhere,
• Concern for the natural environment heightened in recent decades, evolving into a major responsibility for the U.S. mining industry but affecting most foreign competitors to a lesser degree,
• It was realized that the safety and health standards of the prewar period were no longer acceptable. While this has been most serious for coal, it has also affected metal mining costs.

As a result of these factors, present mining technologies (with a few exceptions) are designed to achieve high labor productivity and to handle large volumes of rock or ore. Mining machines, especially those used in surface mines, have huge capacities but very high unit capital costs. This mining technology was developed and implemented mainly in the United States for metal and surface coal mining. Mass production technology for

A continuous miner unit, together with the Longwall system, represents the forefront of mechanization in underground coal mining. (Courtesy M.D.G. Salamon, Colorado School of Mines.)

underground coal mining (i.e., room and pillar mining) was also initially developed in the United States. Longwall technology, which is regarded by many as the most effective underground coal mining method and which will form most of the basis of future development, was imported from Europe.

Limitations of Present Mining Technology

Virtually every mechanized mining system used today was in use by the late 1950s. Recent advances have been limited to increasing the size of the equipment and to a few improvements to achieve higher labor productivity. This approach provided only limited opportunities for continued improvement. This policy of evolutionary equipment development has resulted in a situation where most foreign companies use technology identical to that used by their U.S. counterparts, placing the U.S. companies at a disadvantage because of lower ore grades and higher environmental protection costs and unit labor costs, which although improved, may still be higher than those of competitors.

The Case for New Technology

The recent return to profitability by many mining companies resulted from their own cost-cutting efforts and from rises in the prices of many mineral commodities. This improvement has created a favorable opportunity to invest in the future of the industry through development of new technologies. The present evolution of mining equipment may be leading to a dead end; if real progress is to be made, the mining industry must embark on a new research program that will result in mining systems that will reduce demands placed on the abilities of operators, remove operators as far as possible from dangerous environments, and exploit opportunities created by minimizing the need for humans in mines.

Since many of the ground support systems and environmental measures used in the mining industry are designed primarily to protect human beings, the absence of workers would create opportunities for redesigning mining processes. In other words, new technologies (e.g., robotics and automation) should not merely reduce the labor force but also exploit the opportunities presented by an operator-free working environment.

Directions for Future R&D

By its nature, mining involves intimate interaction with the rock mass. Unfortunately, geological conditions are variable and unpredictable by available means on the scales relevant here. A mining system must therefore have substantial cognitive abilities to recognize and react to unpredictable varia-

At San Manuel Copper Mine in Arizona, underground trains are controlled by a radio dispatcher from the surface. (Courtesy Magma Copper Company.)

tions. Currently, the trained and experienced operator provides all cognitive abilities. If the operator's burden is to be eased and mining automation is to become a reality, more and more cognitive ability will have to be imparted to the inanimate part of the system. A number of obstacles hamper the development of intelligent mining systems. Some of these are fundamental and confront the designers of any automated system that must operate in unpredictable conditions (e.g., space or battlefield autonomous vehicles). Others are intimately related to mining (e.g., fragmentation of rock, prediction of variations in the geological environment, navigation in a confined underground space). It seems logical to assume that mining research will have to solve its specific problems, accessing data from other fields by soliciting the aid of high-technology companies with related experience.

Four areas of research can be identified that address the problems to be overcome if a new generation of mining systems is to be realized:

• Geosensing, or the ability to (1) predict variation in the ore body, (2) sense the closeness of geological disturbances (e.g., faults), and (3) obtain in situ measurements of grade variations, would improve the likelihood of discovering new deposits and contribute to the design of more effective mining equipment. The feasibility of automated mining relies on this data for the navigation and control of an intelligent system. Although clearly related to aspects of geophysics and geochemistry, this research area must aim for resolution and accuracy that has not hitherto been attempted.

• Nonexplosive rock fragmentation would be a great advantage to the mining industry and is a basic component of automated mining systems. Considerable advances have been made in recent decades in the mechanical extraction of softer rocks, especially in the area of hydraulic mining. Nonexplosive extraction offers enhanced safety through better control and continuity of operations, leading to improved production capacities.

• Intelligent mining systems incorporating advanced levels of cognitive ability in inanimate components of the system would allow new approaches in mining and reduce the exposure of operators to hostile working environments.

• In situ mining is a potentially revolutionary mining method that could greatly improve mining economies and allow a human-free working environment, exploitation of low-grade mineral resources, and retention of waste underground.

MINERAL PROCESSING TECHNOLOGIES

Current Mineral Processing Technologies

Mineral processing has a critical role in determining the yield and quality of concentrates for smelting or other product preparation steps. Most current mineral processing technologies were invented (if not implemented) in the nineteenth century (see Table 3-1). For example, the two crusher types now in use (jaw and gyratory) were nineteenth-century developments; they have both increased in size, capacity, and effectiveness since then, but they are unchanged in principle. The cone crusher, a product of the 1920s, is only a modification of the gyratory design. The ball mill, brought to this country from Germany shortly after the turn of the century, has increased substantially in size, but its basic design and action are unchanged.

Concentration by gravity in its earliest forms involved stratification by differential settling. New types of gravity washers were introduced in the nineteenth century and achieved relatively higher efficiencies with improved designs of many of the older devices. More importantly, mechanization was added. Dependence on gravity methods alone for concentration was relieved by the invention of magnetic separators, again in the nineteenth century, and electrostatic separation, also patented in the nineteenth century but first applied in 1907. Flotation, with early patents in the late nineteenth century, had its first use in Australia in 1906 and in the United States in 1911, and almost every reagent type in current use had been established by 1926.

Directions for Future R&D

The energy inefficiency of the comminution or pulverizing process has been known for over a century, yet there have been no major developments

TABLE 3-1 Chronology of Major Innovations in Milling, Nineteenth and Twentieth Centuries

Comminution	
Stamps	Described by Agricola and operated then by water power; mechanized in the nineteenth century, first by steam and later by electric power.
Roll crusher	Invented in England (1806); introduced to the continent (1832).
Jaw crusher	Patented in U.S. by Blake (1858); first use (1861); introduced to Europe (before 1866).
Gyratory	First competitive trial versus jaw crusher by Gates (1883).
Ball mill	Invented by Bruckner in Germany (1876); earliest on ores in U.S. 1905.
Autogenous grinding	First use Kalgoorlie (1890s); South Africa (1906); development period North America (1945–1955).
Classification and sizing	Mechanical classifier (about 1905).
	Cyclone (early 1930s).
	DSM sieve bend (ca. 1960).
Concentration	
Gravity	Wilfley Table (patented 1896); in wide use (by 1900).
	Heavy medium separation (on ores) (1930s).
	Heavy medium cyclone (late 1930s).
	Humphreys spiral (first used about 1943).
Electrical	
Magnetic separation	Cleaning apatite by magnetite removal (1853).
	Ball-Norton belt separator produced 1,000 tons of magnetite concentrates (1888).
	High-intensity wet separator (ca. 1960).
Electrostatic separation	Nonmineral applications (1879).
	First successful use on ores: sphalerite-pyrite (1907).
Flotation	First conception: Bessel brothers (1877).
	First use: Australia (1905) of Potter Delprat process, in the United States (1911).
	First use of soluble collectors: Martin (1915).
	Controlled selectivity: Sheridan and Griswold cyanide (1922).
	Fatty acid collectors: Christensen (1923).

SOURCE: Art iler (64).

Early test flotation cell, Montana, circa 1915. (Courtesy N. Arbiter.)

Laboratory flotation test to produce a sulfide mineral concentrate containing cobalt, 1988. (Courtesy Bureau of Mines, Albany Research Center.)

in this technology. Except for blasting and the potential applications of alternative energy forms, comminution depends entirely on conversion of electrical energy to motion in crushing or grinding machinery. The low-head aspects of the tumbling mill, as well as the indirect nature of its energy transformations, suggest the possible use of other forms of energy that can be applied more directly for producing ore fragmentation. This is related to another aspect of fragmentation that has been almost entirely neglected in conventional comminution theory but that is the starting point for theories of fracture, namely the existence of flaws (ranging from in situ structural faults in a mine before blasting, through cracks formed during blasting, to grain boundaries and lattice defects or dislocations) that influence subsequent grinding efficiency. Exploitation of these flaws should be a major goal of comminution research.

There is a marked analogy between problems of improving efficiencies in comminution and flotation. Both systems involve interaction between relevant properties of the materials processed and dynamic characteristics of processing machinery. With both, machine evolution has had the goal of providing for a number of functions, often with different requirements, in a single unit. As a result there must be a compromise with less than optimum execution of all functions. This compromise is evident in the mechanical flotation cell. The critical requirements are to provide optimum conditions both for stable particle/bubble attachment and for gravity separation of bubbles from pulp. A third requirement, related only indirectly to the process itself, is the necessity of providing sufficient flow velocities to keep all coarse fractions in suspension within the particle/bubble contacting zones. Flotation can be optimized through developing the most effective device for maintaining as well as obtaining particle/bubble contact and designing the optimum phase separator to receive the discharge from the mixer.

Although there have been claims and counterclaims for collectorless flotation of sulfide minerals as far back as the 1930s, it is only within the past few years that the phenomenon has moved out of the laboratory and into positive demonstrations in pilot-plant and full-scale circuits. Results have been encouraging, but limited scope and proprietary factors do not allow for firm economic evaluation. Nevertheless, significant benefits are anticipated in the treatment of porphyry copper ores, which appear to be most readily amenable to this treatment.

METAL EXTRACTION TECHNOLOGIES

Metal extraction technologies transform ores and mineral concentrates into salable metal commodities. Virtually all current extraction technologies are based on pyrometallurgical or hydrometallurgical techniques. A few exceptions do exist, however, such as the carbonyl process route for nickel.

Recent Pyrometallurgical Process Developments

Copper

The U.S. copper industry has largely replaced traditional reverberatory smelting methods with flash smelting processes. Reverberatory and electric furnaces continue to fade under environmental and energy cost pressures, and only one electric furnace is currently in use in the United States. Sulfur emissions from smelters are contained as marketable sulfuric acid and liquid sulfur dioxide (SO_2). Foreign companies are relying primarily on flash smelting, and the flash smelters operating in the United States today are all of foreign design.

Research has focused on the tuyere injection of concentrates into bath smelters and elimination of the converter. Alternatives to the converter are sought that will allow continuous operation and produce constant gas flow at high SO_2 strength. Some significant R&D is being conducted on copper production technology, but overall funding remains modest. The most notable projects are the chloride hydrometallurgy-based Cuprex process, the Norddeutsche Affinerie/Lurgi cyclone smelting process, the Queneau-Schuhmann-Lurgi (QSL) reactor, the ISASMELT process, flash converting of matte, and continuing studies of flash smelting reaction thermodynamics and kinetics. Most of these innovations were made outside the United States, and all were first implemented at foreign operations.

Nickel

Flash and electric furnace smelting produce most of the nickel matte from sulfide concentrates; electric furnaces and leaching dominate lateritic nickel production. Converting of nickel matte is done pyrometallurgically in rotary converters. Technological developments in the 1980s on nickel smelting and refining have focused on increasing energy efficiency and improving environmental control of existing operations and on adopting some of the technologies used in other industries to nickel operations.

Zinc

Roast-leach-electrowin (RLE) technology has improved steadily since its invention in 1913, increasing its dominance of the primary zinc smelting and refining industry in the 1980s. Only about 10 to 15 percent of primary zinc is still produced pyrometallurgically, primarily by the Imperial Smelting Process (ISP) and electrothermic process, both of which require thermal refining to produce special high-grade metal. Environmental pressure on zinc leach residue and steel-making dust disposal, particularly in the United

States and Europe, has stimulated development and improvement of processes that can produce an environmentally acceptable, disposable residue and recover zinc and lead. The use of a lead splash condenser in the ISP has caused that process to come under environmental pressures. Little R&D on zinc production technology has been undertaken during the 1980s other than that directed toward environmental issues. No new primary production processes for zinc have been developed since the 1950s, although some modest work on decreasing energy requirements has led to pilot-scale trials of a hydrogen anode concept in West Germany.

Lead

Most of the world's primary lead is produced by the sinter-blast furnace-kettle refining process. Most secondary lead results from blast furnace, reverberatory furnace, and short rotary furnace smelting of scrap batteries. No integration of primary and secondary technology has yet occurred on a significant commercial scale, although the QSL reactor process has such potential. Environmental pressures (workplace and ambient lead exposure) led to development of significant new smelting technologies overseas in the 1970s and 1980s, but none of these have been adopted in the United States.

Aluminum

Primary aluminum is produced by the Hall-Heroult process, while secondary aluminum is generally produced by simple remelting in induction or

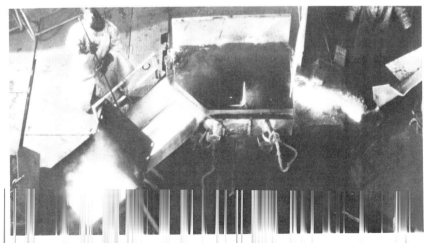

Casting lead bullion at a secondary lead smelter. (Courtesy The Doe Run Company.)

reverberatory furnaces. Recycling of aluminum continues to increase as more aluminum-containing products are made and incentives for recovering aluminum-containing products continue. Since current recycling technology is relatively simple and cost-effective, the committee expects little change in recycling techniques other than development of better methods for sorting aluminum alloys to minimize cross-contamination during reprocessing.

Precious Metals

Roasting has been the primary pyrometallurgical process used for precious metals extraction. A selective roasting technique has been developed at the El Indio mine in Chile for the treatment of arsenic-bearing concentrates, making these materials salable. New roasting technology will also be used at several projects under construction in the United States and Canada, with all gaseous effluents being contained in a cost-effective manner. Circulating fluid bed roasting for processing refractory gold ore, a process adapted from alumina calcining technology, is under investigation for a major overseas project and will be compared to the autoclave processing alternative.

Recent Hydrometallurgical Process Developments

Copper

Major increases in copper production have resulted from the use of solvent extraction/electrowinning processes in the United States and abroad. New reagents have been developed that permit higher extraction efficiency and lower solvent losses due to impurity contamination. New equipment is under development to reduce capital costs and solvent inventory. A technique for high-intensity electrowinning using permanent stainless steel cathodes is also being developed, as is a leaching-solvent extraction/electrowinning process using ferric chloride technology. Ion exchange resins are under investigation for the removal of copper from dilute mine waters.

Conventional electrolytic refining continues to be the workhorse of high-purity copper production. Several refineries using permanent cathodes have now been constructed and more are planned. More refineries are integrating forward to produce continuous cast copper rod.

Nickel and Cobalt

Nickel refining remains dominated by carbonyl technology and electrowinning. No significant new developments have occurred in laterite technology to improve energy efficiency. Concentration technology has not been improved, and the resulting need to process essentially the entire feed remains the major hurdle to be overcome in any effort to make laterite processing

Bulldozers working on copper leach piles at San Manuel Copper Mine in Arizona. (Courtesy Magma Copper Mine.)

naconda refinery thode both, 1902. (Courtesy N. Arbiter.)

Electrowon cathodes being lifted from a cell at San Manuel Copper Mine in Arizona, 1989. (Courtesy Magma Copper Company.)

more competitive with sulfide processing. New reagents have also been developed to permit high separation efficiencies between nickel and cobalt, yet no major new facilities have been constructed to utilize these new reagents.

Zinc

Improvements have continued in the application of the standard zinc flowsheet of roasting, leaching, and electrowinning. In addition, pressure leaching techniques have been introduced to improve recovery and sulfur management in some plants. A pressure leach has replaced roasting in several expansion projects, producing sulfur rather than sulfuric acid as a by-product.

Lead

Significant new developments in primary lead hydrometallurgy are under way in Italy, and plants treating secondary lead may soon be in operation in Europe and the United States.

Aluminum

Virtually all the world's primary aluminum is produced via the well-established and nearly optimized Bayer process for alumina, followed by the Hall-Heroult process for reduction. Several direct reduction and chloride-based processes have been developed and evaluated through pilot-plant scale during the 1970s and 1980s, but none has been reduced to commercial practice. Alternative feed sources for aluminum have been also evaluated, but bauxite remains the primary raw material. Significant R&D has continued into ways to decrease power consumption and improve electrode performance in the existing reduction process and to decrease emissions to the environment, with some success.

Precious Metals

Pressure oxidation of refractory gold ores appears to be the emerging technology of choice where roasting cannot be used. Biooxidation is also being developed. Heap leaching of low-grade ores by cyanide solutions, with or without agglomeration, continues to expand, with gold-bearing solutions being treated by carbon adsorption/desorption units followed by electrowinning. The use of ion exchange resins and solvents to replace carbon is showing promise in the testing stage.

The primary technology for platinum group metals (PGMs) has become electric furnace matte smelting of flotation concentrates followed by matte leaching, chloride-based leaching of matte leach residue, and then separation and purification of the PGMs by classical solvent extraction, precipitation, and/or ion exchange techniques.

Developments in the field of precious metals also include the installation of autoclaves for whole ore oxidation in California, Utah, Nevada, and Brazil. Improvements have been made in the activated carbon process, and high-capacity contactors have been put into operation. Demonstration plants for biological oxidation of pyritic and arsenopyritic gold ores have been constructed in Canada and Africa, and a commercial plant has been built in the United States.

The search for chemical oxidation agents for refractory gold ores continues, with attention focusing on chlorine and nitric acid. These latter reagents appear to offer a major advantage when large quantities of silver are present; silver recovery is poor in currently used roasting and autoclaving processes.

Directions for Future R&

The hydrometallurgical and biotechnological techniques associated with in situ extraction could have a great impact on minerals and mining industry. In situ extraction is an interdisciplinary technique bridging mining, mineral processing, and extraction metallurgy that is currently being used for the production of uranium, copper, salt, potash, and trona. In situ techniques have also been successfully applied to the extraction of borates. Further research into advanced reagents or designed organisms capable of extracting specific metals from underground deposits with a minimum of earth moving and waste production could revolutionize the minerals and metals industry. Before these techniques can be properly and universally applied to in situ extraction methods, however, extensive research is required in the areas of underground and surface fluid control, containment, and dewatering techniques.

Residue processing and waste disposal are problems of increasing importance to the minerals and metals industry. Traditionally, the presence of undesirable impurities has not been given great weight in assessing the value of a mineral deposit. In the United States, however, a significant amount of the effort currently required to bring a mine into production, or to preserve the life of an existing operation, is related to the protection of the work force and the environment. Metallurgists in the domestic industry thus find themselves with an increasingly difficult task: they must produce the highest-quality product to compete in world markets but must also contain completely all of the reagents and effluents and transform any toxic components into useful by-products or harmless wastes. To address the problems of environmental quality and waste disposal, R&D should now be focused on a systems approach to process development. The objective of this approach is to devise processes that do not simply minimize the cost of recovery of the principal mineral values from an ore but that also facilitate the required containments and create harmless wastes at minimum overall cost.

RESEARCH AGENDA

The mining industry is in a state of R&D stagnation. Most of the technologies currently in use were developed at least 20 years ago. The demise of many companies and the restructuring of others to survive the recent decline in commodity prices have made the industry stable for the present, but it is in danger of ignoring its future. If the minerals and metals industry is to survive and flourish into the twenty-first century, new technologies must be developed. The following sections summarize the major conclusions of this chapter and outline the research agenda that will be required to enhance the competitive posture of the U.S. minerals and metals industry.

Exploration

Although the methods of exploration currently in use are generally satisfactory, and considerable strides have been made, even minor further advancements in technology, improvements in data bases, and increased avail-

The world's first plant to biologically degrade cyanide and strip toxic heavy metals from wastewater went into operation in 1985. This technology and the mutant bacteria it uses were developed by Homestake Mining Company. The mine is located in Lead, S.D. (Courtesy Homestake Mining Company.)

ability of information to more companies could dramatically increase both the number of deposits discovered and the competitiveness of the U.S. minerals and metals industry. Evolutionary advances that would improve the current state of exploration techniques are

- improved spatial and spectral image resolution to penetrate foliage and surface cover;
- increased digital geophysical coverage of the United States magnetically, gravitationally, radiometrically, and spectrally to one-half mile; and
- improved drilling/sampling techniques and analytical methods to increase basic knowledge.

A research advance that could revolutionize the U.S. minerals and metals industry would be the elucidation of a more complete general theory of ore genesis and deposition.

Mining Technologies

The mining industry must strive to develop automated mining, processing, and extraction technologies that can be operated and maintained with the minimum exposure of people to difficult or hazardous conditions. Design criteria must include the concept of the clean plant, where all equipment is assessed for its spillage potential and where total containment of harmful residues must be provided. Areas of research needed to address the problems of developing a new generation of mining systems are

• geosensing, or the ability to predict variations in the ore body or the coal seam, sense the closeness of geological disturbances, and obtain in situ measurements of ore grade;
• nonexplosive rock fragmentation;
• intelligent mining systems incorporating advanced levels of cognitive ability; and
• in situ mining, a potentially revolutionary mining method that could greatly improve mining economies and allow a human-free working environment.

Minerals Processing

Radical changes, bordering on revolutionary, may be in prospect for mineral processing:

• in general, through advances in modeling and automation with computer control of operations;
• in comminution, through integration of blasting with crushing, through taking full advantage of preexisting and process-created structural weaknesses, and in the use of energy other than electromechanical; and
• in flotation, through the development of alternative machines that exhibit higher hydraulic and process efficiencies and through advances in the application of collectorless flotation of sulfide minerals.

Metals Extraction

The discovery of hydrometallurgical and biotechnological techniques for in situ extraction could greatly influence the minerals and metals industry. Further research into advanced reagents or designed organisms capable of extracting specific metals from underground deposits, with a minimum of earth moving and waste production, could potentially revolutionize the field. Before in situ extraction methods can be properly and universally applied, however, extensive research is required in the areas of underground and surface fluid control, containment, and dewatering techniques.

R&D should address environmental quality and waste disposal issues through a systems approach as a means of reducing the impact of environmental regulation on competitiveness. Processes must be developed that minimize the cost of recovering metals while at the same time meeting environmental standards, maintaining the required containment for harmful materials, and creating harmless waste at minimum costs.

REFERENCES

Arbiter, N., ed. 1964. *Milling Methods in the Americas.* New York: Columbia University Press.

Huet, G. 1866. *Preparation Mechanique.* Paris.

Office of Technology Assessment (OTA). 1988. *Copper: Technology & Competitiveness.* OTA-*E-368.* Washington, D.C.: U.S. Government Printing Office, p. 119.

Revnivtsev, V. I. 1988. We really need revolution in comminution. In *Proceedings of the XVI International Mineral Processing Congress,* K. S. E. Forssberg, ed. Stockholm: Elsevier, pp. 93-114.

4

Resources for Research and Development

INDUSTRY RESEARCH AND DEVELOPMENT

In the early 1980s, squeezed between stagnating metal prices and rising operating costs, U.S. mineral and metal producers took a number of steps to improve their financial outlook. Their focus was on near-term survival, however, and long-term research and development (R&D) were given very low priority. Corporate R&D facilities were reduced in size or closed, and much of the remaining research was redirected at short-term operational problems and away from long-term or high-risk projects. Expenditures for mining R&D by the metal industry reflect the cutbacks of expenses over the past decade. As shown in Table 4-1, expenditures for internal and contracted R&D declined from $133.5 million in 1980 to $22.5 million in 1988. A similar decline is reflected in the number of personnel committed to the R&D effort.

The U.S. minerals and metals industry includes activities ranging from exploration and primary mining to the manufacture and sale of consumer goods. These activities require a correspondingly broad range of R&D. The points where R&D emphasis is placed at any given time reflect the needs of particular industry segments or even specific companies. Much of the R&D of the aluminum industry, for example, focuses on the production of finished or semifinished goods. Only a small fraction of the approximately $250 million spent by the industry on R&D each year goes toward primary processing. The steel industry, on the other hand, focuses its research efforts on improving the steel-making process. Of the approximately $100

79

TABLE 4-1 Industry Support of Metal
Mining Research and Development

Year	R&D Expenditures ($ millions)	R&D Personnel
1980	133.5	1,735
1985	23.0	—
1986	26.0	—
1987	25.0	—
1988	22.5	365

SOURCE: Expenditure and personnel data for 1980
and 1988 are from T. McNulty, 1989, research and
development in *Materials and Society;* vol. 13, no.
2, pp. 189–191. Expenditure data for 1985–1987
are from the Bureau of the Census, based on the
annual Survey of Industrial Research and Development
conducted for the National Science Foundation;
information on R&D personnel was not available
from the Bureau of the Census.

million spent annually on R&D (approximately 0.25 percent of sales), about
a quarter goes toward improved iron- and steel-making processes. With a
growing share of the steel production capacity in electric furnaces that process
scrap and the decreasing tendency for primary producers to own their own
ores, there is a decline in the emphasis on industry research for the mining
and processing of iron ore.

The domestic base metals (copper, lead, and zinc) are integrated only
from mining through the production of refined products. At one time the
larger companies were involved in finished products like wire and cable,
brass, paint, and chemicals, but today they have all but disappeared through
divestitures and shifts in markets. The base metal producers now depend on
industry groups such as the International Copper Association (ICA), the
Copper Development Association (CDA), and the International Lead-Zinc
Research Organization (ILZRO) for product research. However, membership
in these groups is not universal and budgets are small, generally on the
order of $2 million to $4 million per year. Company-owned research laboratories have been but severely curtailed, and much of the remaining
R&D capability can be found at operating sites where it is quite site
specific and problem oriented.

The gold boom in the United States during the past decade was materially assisted by Bureau of Mines research on heap leaching of very low-grade ores. Most of the Bureau's work was done before the boom really began, and it has been followed by episodes of intensive R&D by individual companies directed at problems posed by specific ore deposits. At the same time, companies that sell goods and services to gold miners have brought forth a steady stream of innovative products, ranging from hydraulic shovels to analytical equipment, which have helped the producers to improve efficiency and lower costs. However, the gold mining industry overall is probably spending less than $7 million annually on R&D, with most of that amount devoted to work on only two problems: gold-bearing refractory sulfide ores and ores containing natural carbonaceous materials.

FEDERAL ROLE IN MINERALS RESEARCH AND DEVELOPMENT

Several agencies of the federal government provide support for mining and minerals research and technology development. They are the

- Department of the Interior (DOI)
  —Bureau of Mines (BOM)
  —U.S. Geological Survey (USGS)
- National Science Foundation (NSF)
- Department of Energy (DOE)
- Department of Commerce (DOC)
  —National Institute of Standards and Technology (NIST)
  —National Oceanic and Atmospheric Administration (NOAA)

The lead agency, accounting for the great majority of federal research funding in this field, is the Department of the Interior through its Bureau of Mines. BOM research programs focus variously on improvements in exploration and mining technology; minerals and materials science and processing technology; health, safety, and environmental technology; and ancillary programs such as methods for improving process management and management technology (e.g., through the use of computer control). The nature of the research ranges from fundamental to highly applied, although the emphasis is strongly toward the applied end. The BOM research is conducted both in-house and at university laboratories.

The U.S. Geological Survey also maintains programs of research under its Office of Mineral Resources. This research involves the theoretical and technical aspects of mineral exploration and resource assessment. It encompasses both geochemical and geophysical methods for locating and modeling mineral deposits in relation to the environments in which they occur. Other projects support the preparation of resource maps and information systems that are valuable exploration tools for industry; this research is carried out through field studies as well as laboratory experimentation. There is some overlap between the USGS and BOM research in support of exploration and economic assessment of mineral deposits.

Another agency providing very modest support for mining and minerals research is the National Science Foundation. Through its Materials Engineering and Processing Program, the NSF funds a small amount of work (under $700,000 in FY 1988) in extraction, smelting, and solidification processes. The Division of Materials Research supports a program of research in metallurgy; however, the program focuses on basic scientific research in physical rather than extractive metallurgy. NSF research in related topics, such as tunneling technology, could benefit the mining industry, but the lack of an infrastructure for the transfer of research results to the mining industry limits the opportunity to apply research from other fields to the needs of the mining industry. The NSF was a source of more substantial funding in the past, but NSF management apparently came to view mining as a "sunset industry" and moved away from it, judging from its responses to mining-related proposals in recent years.

The Department of Energy has more than 20 program offices responsible for aspects of materials research, from basic to applied. In FY 1989, $384 million was spent on materials-related R&D departmentwide, including over $200 million of DOE's $450 million budget for basic energy sciences—the largest single materials research program in the federal government. However, little DOE work is relevant to mining and extraction; much of it is directed at materials science for advanced energy-related materials, and most of the rest concerns processing and refining electronic materials and specialized alloys, uranium, and weapons-grade plutonium. Some of the research with relevance to the present study is connected with the management of nuclear wastes; some is connected with drilling in hot rock to tap geothermal energy.

DOE programs relevant to this study include development for high-temperature applications and corrosion-resistant alloys, conducted at Oak Ridge National Laboratory under sponsorship of the Division of Materials Sciences of the Office of Basic Energy Sciences. Another program, the Steel Initiative under the Office of Industrial Programs, was mandated by Congress in support of the steel industry. It has many facets, including automated process control, continuous casting, and alternative methods of direct extraction of iron from iron ore. This program was expanded to include aluminum and copper by the Steel and Aluminum Energy Conservation and Technology Competitiveness Act of 1988. The DOE has prepared a research plan that identifies specific opportunities for research to contribute to the competitiveness of the steel, aluminum, and copper industries through increased energy efficiency.

The Department of Commerce supports mining and minerals research through two of its agencies, the National Institute of Standards and Technology and the National Oceanic and Atmospheric Administration. NIST currently supports a single project covering the bioactive extraction of metals. Some of its work on sensors for use in processing is planned to be relevant to metals processing. NOAA, through its Sea Grant program, sponsors a limited amount of academic research relating to ocean mining and minerals.

The Department of Defense (DOD) currently sponsors very little research in the areas covered by this study. The Defense Advanced Research Projects Agency, the Strategic Defense Initiative Office, and the military services (particularly the U.S. Air Force) conduct research in advanced materials processing and manufacturing, including physical metallurgy, extrusion, rolling, and joining. The National Aeronautics and Space Administration (NASA) sponsors research in many of the same areas. But none of these materials user agencies (with the possible exception of some scattered research on excavation by the U.S. Army Corps of Engineers) is involved at all in the upstream end of materials.

Other federal agencies do not support significant amounts of R&D in this area, but do provide input into the research programs of the Bureau of Mines and others. These contributing agencies include the Mine Safety and Health Administration, the National Institute for Occupational Safety and Health, the Office of Surface Mining Reclamation and Enforcement, and the Environmental Protection Agency.

Several advisory groups participate in the shaping of government policies with respect to minerals. The National Critical Materials Council (NCMC) is supposed to advise the President on national materials policies and issues. The National Strategic Materials and Minerals Program Advisory Committee has performed a similar function for the Secretary of the Interior. The Committee on Mining and Mineral Resources Research also advises the Secretary of the Interior on a number of matters relating to minerals research, particularly in the Mineral Institutes program. A fourth group, the Committee on Materials (COMAT), functions under the auspices of the Office of Science and Technology Policy in the Executive Office of the President. Through a subcommittee, the Interagency Materials Group, COMAT attempts to enhance cooperation and coordination between agencies involved in the support of materials research. The effectiveness of these advisory groups has been quite mixed. (The subject of mineral policies, including R&D policies, is addressed in Chapter 5.)

Research Resources

The overall R&D resources of the federal government in the minerals and metals field include both the R&D expenditures of the various agencies and the various federal laboratories, including in-house agency laboratories and national laboratories, that may devote all or part of their efforts to R&D in this field. Agency funding of R&D in FY 1989 is presented in Table 4-2. Only the Bureau of Mines is oriented explicitly toward mining and extractive metallurgy; it was difficult to obtain exact budget figures for the other

TABLE 4-2 Federal Expenditures for Mining- and Minerals-Related R&D, 1989 (1989 Appropriation)

Agency/Program	Federal Expenditures ($ thousand)
Bureau of Mines	
Health, Safety, and Mining Technology	51,672[a]
Minerals and Materials Science	24,643[a]
Environmental Technology	14,574[a]
Mineral Institutes and Generic Centers	10,012[b]
TOTAL	100,901
U.S. Geological Survey	
Development of Assessment Techniques	10,000
Strategic and Critical Minerals	3,700[c]
National Mineral Resource Assessment	9,300[c]
TOTAL	23,000
National Science Foundation	669[d,e]
Department of Energy	12,186[f]
National Institute of Standards and Technology	350
National Oceanic and Atmospheric Administration	
Sea Grant Program: Marine Geological Resources	571[d]
Deep Seabed Mining Research	750[a]
TOTAL	14,526
FEDERAL TOTAL	138,427[c]

[a]Includes Bureau of Mines in-house laboratories ($66.3 million in nine labs) plus a variety of externally funded projects in industry and universities.

[b]Does not include $2.35 million for Respirable Dust Generic Center, budgeted as a separate line item under Environmental Technology.

[c]Estimated (1).

[d]1988 amount.

[e]Nine grants (FY 1988) in extraction, smelting, and solidification processes (in Materials Engineering and Processing Program).

[f]Derived from a count of apparently relevant materials R&D projects. (Does not include the so-called Steel Initiative. Authorizations under the Steel and Aluminum Energy Conservation and Technology Competitiveness Act of 1988 are $2 million in 1989, $20 million in 1990, and $25 million in 1991.)

agencies that support R&D in this field, but their involvement is so small that rounded estimates will suffice. Only in the case of DOE are the estimates problematical, and here a conservative estimate was reached by adding the reported budgets of projects that appear relevant. This estimate may ignore a considerable amount of relevant DOE basic research in surface chemistry, thermodynamics, interphase and microstructure studies, and reaction mechanisms.

As noted above, BOM provides the majority of the funding in this area. Figure 4-1 charts appropriations for the Bureau's research throughout the 1980s. Funding, in current dollars, actually declined by several percentage points during the period. Although the R&D budget is now trending upward from the low of 1986, after adjusting for inflation it is still well below the level of a decade ago. Most of this money is spent in BOM's in-house laboratories, although BOM is also a major supporter of academic R&D in this field (see below).

Federal R&D resources also include the extensive federal laboratories, many of which are equipped for basic and applied research in relevant areas. BOM's nine in-house Mining and Metallurgy Laboratories, for example, perform almost half of the research funded by the federal government in these areas. Table 4-3 lists these laboratories, along with their FY 1989 funding levels and primary areas of specialization. Also relevant to R&D needs in the minerals and metals industry are some of the national laboratories. Oak Ridge National Laboratory, for example, conducts research in metallurgy, metals characterization, and processing theory. A primary focus of this research program, which totaled between $25 million and $30 million in FY 1989, is high-temperature alloys such as nickel aluminides. Argonne

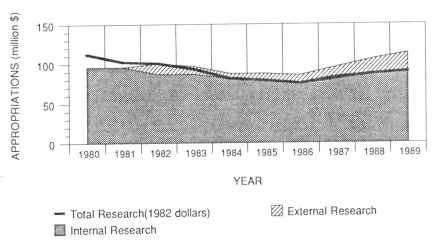

FIGURE 4-1 Bureau of Mines research budgets, 1980-1989. Source: Bureau of Mines.

TABLE 4-3 Bureau of Mines Mining and Metallurgy Laboratories

Research Center	FY 1989 Funding	Research Specialties
Albany Research Center	$7,244,000	Minerals characterization; materials science; pyro-, hydrometallurgy; recycling; wear and corrosion; refractory metals
Denver Research Center	5,362,000	Underground mine design; theoretical rock mechanics; prediction and control of failures/hazards; geomechanical field data collection; microseismic monitoring; modeling of rock
Pittsburgh Research Center	24,446,000	Mine explosions; dust and noise control; subsidence prediction and control; acid mine drainage prediction and control; electrical safety; mine automation; survival and rescue; expert systems and artificial intelligence; safety; ventilation
Reno Research Center	3,258,000	Electro-, pyro-, and hydrometallurgy; precious metals; microwave technology; rare earths; superalloy scrap recycling; complex sulfide treatment; magnets; catalysts; bioleaching
Rolla Research Center	2,923,000	Electro-, hydro-, and pyrometallurgy
Salt Lake City Research Center	4,627,000	Hydrometallurgy; beneficiation; supercritical fluid solvent systems; waste treatment; brine chemistry; column flotation; advanced materials extraction; in situ mining solution treatment
Spokane Research Center	5,764,000	Rock and soil mechanics; hydrogeology and geochemistry; mining methods; waste management; subsidence control; deep mine design
Tuscaloosa Research Center	3,383,000	Beneficiation; hydrometallurgy; minerals waste treatment; comminution/turbomilling; expert systems for processing
Twin Cities Research Center	9,275,000	In situ mining technology; blasting and drilling technology; equipment safety; seabed mining; mechanical and thermal fragmentation; subsidence; fire protection; hydrology

SOURCE: Data provided by Bureau of Mines.

National Laboratory conducts research in support of the downstream processing of materials to meet specialized needs of the laboratory. This work amounts to about $1 million to $2 million per year in electrochemistry and other specialized processing techniques. Argonne also supports the DOE Steel Initiative through research in continuous casting and chill casting using magnetic confinement. Similarly, Los Alamos National Laboratory conducts some research in hot-rock boring that has relevance for in situ fragmentation and solution mining; the Idaho National Engineering Laboratory performs some $3 million/year in Bureau of Mines research; and other laboratories, such as Pacific Northwest Laboratory, carry out small amounts of research in this field.

Taken together, the national laboratories are a resource of great potential, now only partially tapped, for the performance of research that could improve mining, extraction, and metals processing technologies and their use in industry. That resource includes state-of-the-art facilities, people, and experience in working with a variety of governmental agencies and industry. The DOE Work-for-Others Order requires permission to exceed 20 percent of the work at a DOE laboratory being done for a sponsor other than DOE; however, the work must be consistent with the laboratory's mission. Work for the Nuclear Regulatory Commission is outside this guideline. Other federal laboratories, in particular those of the DOD and NASA, offer a similar potential; however, these laboratories (such as the Air Force Materials Laboratory and the NASA Lewis Research Center) do not appear to be involved in any such research at present.

ACADEMIC RESEARCH RESOURCES AND CAPABILITIES

U.S. preeminence in most technological fields has traditionally rested on the base of research conducted at colleges and universities. In most engineering fields, both basic and applied academic research have been important stimulants to progress in industry. Academic R&D capabilities are also important for the infusion of state-of-the-art concepts into engineering education, whose graduates bring new ideas and approaches into industrial practice. In the mining-related fields, however, the connection between academic R&D and industrial practice has been poor. There are serious questions about both the relevance of university research in these fields and the ability of the industry to assimilate and apply the research results.

Academic Capabilities

The limited infrastructure for industrial R&D in this field is matched by limitations in academic capabilities. Measures of the strength of the academic research infrastructure include the number of university programs and the number of faculty teaching in those programs. Table 4-4 shows the number of academic programs and faculty members in six disciplines that directly support the minerals and metals industry. In formulating the totals some informed judgment was necessary to estimate the content of programs and overlaps between them. This was particularly difficult to do in the case of metallurgical engineering, because the subdiscipline of primary interest, extractive metallurgy, is often not distinguished from physical metallurgy within most program descriptions. The distribution of academic programs by institution is shown in Table 4-5. Several conclusions can be drawn from the information in these tables:

• There are far more programs and faculty devoted to exploration (geological and geophysical engineering) and mining (42 programs and 275 faculty members) than to extractive metallurgy and mineral processing (15 programs and 52 faculty members). The latter numbers appear inadequate to meet the nation's needs across all the metals subindustries.

• The average number of faculty members per program (5.5) is small. Many are not tenured. It is difficult to attract high-quality students and funding, or to conduct coherent and stable programs of research, within such a limited group. As a result, the faculties overall tend to fall below the "critical mass" needed to maintain secure programs. This helps to explain why very few of the programs in these disciplines represent full departments.

• In terms of geographic distribution the great majority of the programs are located in the Midwest and West, near the regions with metal mining and processing operations. This means that many high-quality prospective engineering students from the East no longer come in contact with programs in mining and metals processing.

TABLE 4-4 Academic Programs and Faculty by Fields, 1989

Field	Programs	Faculty
Geological engineering	19	150
Geophysical engineering	3	17
(Extractive) metallurgical engineering	9	30
Mineral processing engineering	6	22
Mining engineering	20	108
Mineral economics	6	20
TOTALS	63	347

SOURCE: E. Ashworth, J. Schanz, personal communications, 1989.

TABLE 4-5 Academic Programs in Mining and Minerals, by Institution

Institution	Geology	Geophysical Engineering	Mineral Processing	Extractive Metallurgy	Mining Engineering	Mineral Economics
University of Alabama				Y	X	
University of Alaska, Fairbanks	X		X		X	
University of Arizona	X				X	X
Arizona State University	X					
University of California, Berkeley		X	X		X	
Colorado School of Mines	X	Y		X	Y	Y
Columbia University					X	
University of Idaho	X			X	X	
University of Kentucky					Y	
Michigan Technological University	X		X		Y	X
University of Minnesota	X			X		
University of Mississippi	X					
University of Missouri, Rolla	Y			Y	Y	
Montana College of Mining Science and Technology[a]	X	X	X		X	
University of Nevada, Reno	X			X	Y	
New Mexico Institute of Mining and Technology	X			X	X	
New Mexico State University	X					
University of North Dakota	X					

TABLE 4-5 Continued

Institution	Geology	Geophysical Engineering	Mineral Processing	Extractive Metallurgy	Mining Engineering	Mineral Economics
Pennsylvania State University	X		X[b]		X	Y
[Pr]inceton University	X					
South Dakota School of Mines				Y	Y	
[and Techn]ology						
Southern Illinois University					Y	
[at Carbon]dale						
University of Texas, Austin	X					X
University of Utah	X			Y	Y	
Virginia Polytechnic Institute and State University					X	
Washington State University	X					
West Virginia University	X		X[b]		Y	Y
University of Wisconsin, Madison	X					
University of Wyoming					X	
Total Programs (63), by discipline	19	3	6	9	20	6

NOTES: X denotes programs that are combined with others to form a department (e.g., Geology/Geological Engineering Department or Mining combined with Petroleum to form a Mineral Engineering Department). Y denotes programs comprising a separate department (often very small).

[a] Montana Tech had separate departments with department heads but has recently reorganized to have one division head with separate programs.

[b] Mainly coal processing.

SOURCES: Society for Mineral Engineering "Guide to Mineral Schools;" E. Ashworth; J. Schanz.

These numbers do not reflect the changes in academic programs over time, particularly the significant decrease in undergraduate programs. Of 26 such programs in 1980, only 20 remain, and 5 of the programs were lost just since 1986. Of the remaining 20 programs, 3 or 4 are in jeopardy because of critically low enrollments and lack of financial support. The Pennsylvania State University, for example, had only one freshman mining engineering student in the spring of 1989; the Colorado School of Mines had 8; Columbia University (designated as a Mineral Institute) had none. To maintain accreditation an engineering program must have at least 4 faculty members devoted to undergraduate teaching. Accreditation is granted by the Accreditation Board for Engineering and Technology and is a crucial determinant of program quality in the eyes of most employers, prospective students, and university administrators. With low enrollment some schools have had to combine departments or programs, and the declining number of faculty members may threaten accreditation, which would further endanger the remaining university programs.

More importantly, declining enrollments and limited research funds have forced most academic investigators either to focus on their established domains, producing small advances in conventional areas, or to switch their focus to new areas outside the minerals and metals industry where greater funding is available. Both responses have reduced the research results available to the mining industry and further increased the separation between academe and industry.

The U.S. minerals and metals industry has benefited greatly from academic research in the past. In rock mechanics, for example, fundamental studies on the failure modes of materials led to useful applications in mine design and excavation equipment design. Research in geologic modeling has advanced exploration technology, and in mineral processing industrial applications have resulted from fundamental work at universities on comminution, minerals beneficiation, electrochemistry, solvent extraction and ion exchange, and thermodynamics. Computer science applications have led to a wealth of technology for operations research, modeling, and mine design, and mineral economics research has greatly improved the forecasting of supply and demand, commodity prices, and other business factors. In the health and safety area, academic research has led to important advances in respirable dust control technology and electromechanical technology in the mine; in the environmental area, academic research has led to substantial advances in mine hydrology, acid mine drainage, sediment control, and vegetation/revegetation. In recent years, however, academic research in the mining and minerals field has tended to be more scientific and theoretical in nature, with less attention to practical engineering contributions. Such contributions are essential if university-developed knowledge and technology are to contribute to the competitiveness of the U.S. industry.

Research Centers and Institutions

The Bureau of Mines, like other mission agencies, supports research at universities on topics relevant to its mission. Under its Mineral Institutes Program, BOM sponsors a number of State Mining and Mineral Resources Research Institutes (referred to as Mineral Institutes) and Generic Mineral Technology Centers (GMTCs). Currently there are 32 Mineral Institutes located in 32 states (see Table 4-6). Each institute functions as an administrative mechanism for the distribution of funds to academic departments for research in the mineral sciences and engineering. The overall budget of the program, which includes both Mineral Institutes and GMTCs, was $10 million in 1989.

BOM makes allotment grants to the institutes based on a 2-for-1 matching of nonfederal (usually state) funds with federal funds. In 1988 the grant was the same—$138,000—for each institute, for a total of $4.4 million. All the universities achieved the necessary matching amounts. About $1.5 million of the allotment grant funding was used to support 269 graduate students (in full or in part) and 99 undergraduate scholarships; additional allotments supported 187 research miniprojects.

In addition to allotment grants, research grants are also made to six GMTCs covering major aspects of the minerals industry. The GMTCs are located at universities with Mineral Institutes and are intended to facilitate

TABLE 4-6 Bureau of Mines Mineral Institutes

1.	University of Alabama	17.	University of Missouri, Rolla
2.	University of Alaska, Fairbanks	18.	Montana College of Mineral Science and Technology
3.	University of Arizona		
4.	University of California, Berkeley	19.	University of Nevada, Reno
5.	Colorado School of Mines	20.	New Mexico Institute of Mining and Technology
6.	Georgia Institute of Technology		
7.	University of Idaho	21.	Columbia University
8.	Southern Illinois University	22.	University of North Dakota
9.	Purdue University	23.	Ohio State University
10.	Iowa State University	24.	University of Oklahoma
11.	University of Kentucky	25.	Pennsylvania State University
12.	Louisiana State University	26.	South Dakota School of Mines
13.	Massachusetts Institute of Technology	27.	University of Texas
		28.	University of Utah
14.	Michigan Technological University	29.	Virginia Polytechnic Institute and State University
15.	University of Minnesota	30.	University of Washington
16.	University of Mississippi	31.	West Virginia University
		32.	University of Wyoming

government-industry-university cooperation and research in each generic area. Each GMTC has a lead institution to coordinate research, provide for seminars, and operate a reference center that disseminates research results. A number of affiliate institutions (all Mineral Institutes) are associated with each GMTC. Table 4-7 lists the six GMTCs, their focus areas, and the lead institutions. In 1989, 93 separate research projects were supported by the GMTCs. Budgets of the centers average about $1 million each, for a total of $7.95 million in 1989. Of this amount, the Respirable Dust Center, at Pennsylvania State University, has $2.35 million budgeted as a separate line item. The other five GMTCs shared some $5.2 million in funding in 1989, with an additional $400,000 used for administrative purposes—for a total of $5.6 million. The independent Mined Lands Reclamation Center, with the University of West Virginia as the lead institution, resembles the GMTCs in structure but is not part of the Mineral Institutes/GMTC program; its $1.5 million funding is included under the Bureau of Mines's Environmental Technology program area.

Research in undersea minerals is conducted under the National Sea Grant

TABLE 4-7 Bureau of Mines Generic Mineral Technology Centers

Mine Systems Design and Ground Control
Lead institution: Virginia Polytechnic Institute and State University
    Covers conditions from permafrost to tropics; fuels, nonmetallics, metals, brines, and open pit and underground mines

Comminution
Lead institution: University of Utah
    Crushing and grinding

Mineral Industry Waste Treatment and Recovery
Lead institution: University of Nevada, Reno
    Fumes, dusts, liquid and solid wastes

Pyrometallurgy
Lead institution: University of Missouri, Rolla
    Applies high temperatures to mineral processes such as smelting, refining, and alloying

Respirable Dust
Lead institution: Pennsylvania State University
    Concerned with particles causing diseases

Marine Mineral Technology
Lead institution: University of Mississippi
    Manganese and phosphate crust mining; sampling and measurement

SOURCE: Information provided by Bureau of Mines.

College Program of the National Oceanic and Atmospheric Administration. Twelve Sea Grant institutions conduct research in areas relevant to mining and minerals, such as undersea minerals characterization and surveys. As with the Mineral Institutes program, the administration has recommended that funding for the Sea Grant program be ended, but the funds have been restored by Congress. NOAA also has a Deep Seabed Mining Research Program that conducts mainly environmental research related to mining of nodules on the ocean floor. Federal research funding in these two programs totals about $1.3 million.

The U.S. Geological Survey sponsors a program of State Water Resources Research Institutes at universities. This program resembles the Mineral Institutes program in its structure and operation. Some of these institutes address problems relevant to mineral resources, such as acid mine drainage and the uses of water in mining operations.

ISSUES AFFECTING FUTURE RESEARCH AND DEVELOPMENT

Industrial Issues

In the minerals and metals industry, where profit margins are generally low, uncertainties over the costs and effectiveness of new technology are potent barriers to support of R&D and the implementation of new technology. While successful implementation of a new technology may be anticipated to increase the profitability of a firm by a limited amount, the potential costs (e.g., the impact of delays as technologies are debugged, the possibility that a technology fails to meet its performance specifications, and the cost of modifying systems to deal with unanticipated problems) may be viewed as a threat not only to the firm's profit margin but also to its competitiveness or even its survival. As a result, incremental technological advances are common, but firms do not put a high priority on the development of major new mining or processing technologies.

In times when they are capital rich, mining companies have secured new deposits rather than invest in the development of new technology. Such a strategy ensures that the benefits of success (i.e., the discovery of a valuable new deposit) are captured by the firm, unlike a technological advantage that may eventually be acquired by competitors, but the difficulty, cost, and high failure rate of exploration for new high-grade deposits limits the value of this approach, particularly in the United States and other industrialized countries that have already been heavily explored.

It is easiest to introduce major new technologies when an industry is new and rapidly expanding and when investment capital is readily available. Considering these factors, domestic mining and metals firms have been at a disadvantage relative to mining operations in developing countries. However, under the pressure of depressed metal prices and new environmental restrictions, the domestic industry did make a rapid and widespread adoption of hydrometallurgical technology. While driven by financial and regulatory pressures, the speed of the shift was due in part to the demonstration that the technology was effective and dependable and that it could be implemented with little risk.

Even the success of the adoption of hydrometallurgy by the copper industry reveals a problem in industry R&D. The solvent extraction/electrowinning technology that the industry adopted was based on research that was conducted for the processing of uranium. While there are many problems that are common to broad segments of the mining and metals industry, there is no industrywide effort to deal with them. In this industry there is no advanced industry research center (equivalent to Bell Laboratories or IBM Research Laboratories) that can afford to remain committed to substantial programs of research over a long period. Nor is there a consortium such as the Electric Power Research Institute or Gas Research Institute to conduct industrywide R&D. In fact, much of the innovative research for the minerals industry is done by companies that are not directly involved in mining and metallurgy but rather in sensors and automatic process controls. As a result, the minerals and metals industry does not have a dependable source of technology to meet its future needs.

Weaknesses and Limitations of Academic Research

The limited funding for the Mineral Institutes program, distributed across many institutions, results in a large number of small uncoordinated projects. The research projects funded through the Mineral Institutes program represent an average of less than three projects at each institute and far less than $30,000 per project. With such small projects, research tends to focus on incremental contributions rather than on revolutionary opportunities to improve technology.

In general, academic research in some of the disciplines may not address the immediate problems of the mining and metals industry. For example, some research in geological and geophysical engineering focuses on areas such as earthquake prediction and underground nuclear waste storage that are not central to the needs of the minerals and metals industry. Because of the dwindling number of programs and faculty and limited research funding, the technological pipeline is emptying. As the research base declines, it will become more difficult to reestablish vigorous programs of research relevant to the needs of the industry. An even more fundamental problem, however, is the lack of an adequate base in the geophysical and geochemical sciences relevant to mining and extraction technology. This work has simply not been done. For example, with most of the major equipment used in rock fragmentation having been developed 100 to 150 years ago, it is possible that new basic science (i.e., increased understanding of fracture mechanisms) could disclose an entirely different approach to fragmentation.

Bureau of Mines-Supported Programs

The university research programs supported by the Bureau of Mines also show some serious problems. Projects conducted through the Mineral Institutes are not subject to peer review (although peer review is instituted on occasion), and the institutes themselves are reviewed against criteria that are specified in the authorizing act but that are not technical in nature (the emphasis is on "eligibility" for the program, and all existing institutes appear routinely to pass the review). The committee has the impression that the geographical and political distribution of institutes and program funds may be the most important consideration in allocating them. The administration has not supported the Mineral Institutes program and has deleted the program from its budget request for the past several years, on the grounds that "this program is no longer an appropriate use of federal funds." Congress has consistently restored funding for the program.

The funding for this program is hardly substantial. Indeed, at $138,000 per school it is distributed so thinly that it has only a minor impact on research. Most engineering programs today require $50,000 to $60,000 to support one graduate student, so at best each Mineral Institute may support two or three full-time equivalent fellowships through federal funds. As a result, many of the 269 graduate students, equivalent to an average of 8.4 per institute, must be supported by matching state and industry funds. Since there were 858 graduate students enrolled in mining- and minerals-related disciplines in 1988, funding by the Bureau of Mines provides at least partial support for 31 percent of the total. Thus, the program's effect is probably greater on education than on research, which may provide a partial justification for its continuation.

The GMTCs present a somewhat stronger picture. The mining industry in general sees them as pursuing more immediately relevant research than do the Mineral Institutes. But there are obvious gaps in coverage; for example, there are no GMTCs covering hydrometallurgy, mining technology, or fine particle processing. Research review is also a problem. The Department of the Interior's Committee on Mining and Mineral Resources Research (CMMRR)—a committee mandated by Congress to advise the Secretary of the Interior on the implementation of the Mineral Institutes program—has evaluated the five original GMTCs every year since they were established in 1984; however, these reviews have been based on reports submitted by the GMTCs, without systematic or rigorous site visits, and the evaluating committee has routinely recommended continuation of all five with equal priority. Because the GMTCs represent a considerable and concentrated investment of scarce federal research funds in this area, review of their programs deserves more careful attention.

Cross-Cutting Issues

To be effective, R&D must draw on both the theoretical strengths of the academic community and the practical knowledge of the industry. Government also has an integral role in promoting R&D on specific matters of public concern and broader interests of international competitiveness and national security. Two issues of importance to the future of minerals and metals R&D cut across the boundaries between industry, academe, and government: transfer of technology and development of a base of trained personnel for the research and operational needs of the industry.

Technology Transfer

A healthy situation in a technology-based field is for university researchers to expand the fundamental science base in a systematic way while performing a limited amount of research with an applied focus. Research results are communicated to industrial laboratories through frequent and substantive technical contacts between academic researchers and their industry counterparts, who then carry the process forward with advanced R&D of competitive processes and products.

This pattern is not evident in the minerals and metals field. With so few academic programs and faculty and so little research funding, academic research as a whole offers little of interest to industry. At the same time the industrial R&D infrastructure is now far too weak to provide a cadre of researchers who could interact effectively with faculty on a nationwide basis. Where such a gap exists between academic research and its industrial application, the technology often cannot be transferred. In many cases, for example, the technology requires large-scale, expensive, proof-of-principle experiments that lend themselves well to neither university research nor industrial plants. In addition, both academic research programs and potential industry users of academic research are scattered at dozens of independent sites with limited communication. This technology-transfer gap between universities and industry is a major barrier to the improvement of competitiveness through technology in the minerals and metals industry.

Human Resource Issues

Another factor affecting the current and future competitiveness of the minerals and metals industry is the availability of qualified engineers, especially

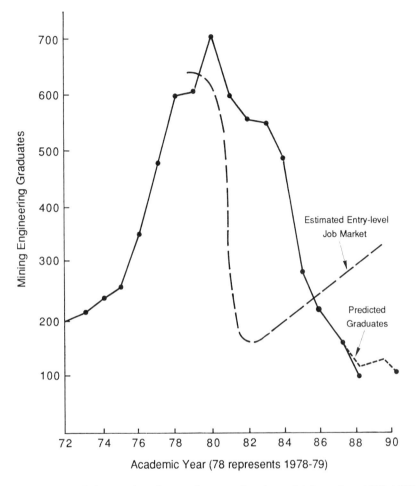

FIGURE 4-2 Mining engineering graduates and estimated job market, 1972-1990. Source: Information provided by E. Ashford, South Dakota School of Mines and Technology.

recent graduates who could bring new technological capabilities to bear on exploration, mining, and extraction operations. The supply of engineering graduates in relevant disciplines has shrunk drastically over the past decade. The decrease in the number of academic programs, described earlier, is a reaction to this drop in student enrollments.

Perhaps the most serious decline has been seen in mining engineering. In 1978 there were 3,117 undergraduate students enrolled in mining engineering nationwide, of whom 850 were freshmen; in 1988 there were 560 undergraduates, with 142 freshmen. In 1981, 702 B.S. degrees in mining engineering were conferred; in 1988 the number was 141, and only 100 students nationwide are expected to graduate with B.S. degrees in mining engineering in 1990. As a case in point, for the first time since its program began, there were no mining engineering graduates at the University of Idaho in May 1988 (Society of Mining Engineering, 1989).

Figure 4-2 compares the number of mining engineering graduates and the number of entry-level jobs since 1972. It appears that a turnaround has just begun in mining engineering enrollments, but the increase is not yet reflected in the number of graduates, and, given attrition rates and the current low output of B.S. mining engineers, the supply of graduates is projected to fall short of industry demand for the predictable future. Anecdotal reports suggest that mining companies were more aggressive than ever in recruiting 1989 graduates, even utilizing headhunters in some cases. As entry-level salaries become more attractive (reported as $33,000 for mining engineers at many companies in 1989), most B.S. graduates leave for industry and few enter graduate school to train for careers in research and education.

REFERENCE

Society of Mining Engineering. 1989. *Minerals Program Data. SME Guide to Minerals Schools.*

5

Federal Role in Technology and Competitiveness

Competitiveness in the minerals and metals industry hinges on many factors, including labor costs, taxes, ore grades, exchange rates, the cost of capital, subsidies, tariffs, and technology for mining and mineral processing. In some cases the U.S. industry is at a disadvantage, in others an advantage. Some other nations (Japan and West Germany, for example) have higher labor costs than U.S. companies, and many foreign producers have higher tax rates than their U.S. counterparts. Indeed, in copper, lead, and zinc the U.S. industry has a smaller tax burden than many foreign producers. Furthermore, exchange rates and interest rates fluctuate sharply and unpredictably. While many of these factors are difficult or impossible to change, the introduction of new technology can have a significant impact on the competitiveness of domestic minerals and metals operations. To be effective, however, a constant commitment of support is required to maintain a technology-based competitive advantage.

There is serious question as to whether the industry supports enough research and development (R&D) to apply and maintain technology as an advantage. As discussed in Chapter 4, U.S. mining companies have cut back their R&D activities and are currently conducting almost no long-term research. In general, the short time horizon (often much less than 10 years) of corporate managers in publicly traded companies may limit their commitment to long-term R&D. By the time the metal markets showed dramatic improvement in 1986-1987, many mining companies had dropped out of cooperative R&D ventures operated through the industrial associations because they believed they no longer needed them. Most prefer to explore for new deposits rather than support R&D—the payoffs perceived as being more predictable and secure. Certainly, no U.S. companies are currently known to be pursuing research on high-risk, high-return, breakthrough technologies on their own initiative.

Industry's disinclination to pursue R&D can be viewed as a market failure in which short-term financial interests overshadow the long-term interests of a company in an international market. Because of this the industry does not adequately reinvest in the technology base on which its own future—and its future ability to satisfy broader national interests—partly depends. While this problem is not limited to the minerals and metals industry, it is more acute for this industry because the connection between basic research in universities and applications in industry is very tenuous and is not systematically supported by either party. In addition, the benefits from R&D to a firm that undertakes or underwrites it are quickly shared by other firms and nations, reducing the competitive advantage to the company funding the research.

At present the federal role in this industry is most evident in policies and actions (e.g., fiscal, monetary, trade, and regulatory) that often complicate and frustrate the industry's competitive situation and make it more difficult for U.S. firms to launch or support long-term R&D programs. Several considerations suggest that this role should change:

- The minerals and metals industry is relatively small, but it is crucial to national interests that are not met by market operations.
- It is highly fragmented, making it difficult to take collective aggressive action on its own behalf.
- The business cycles in the industry are short and deep, making it difficult for companies to sustain long-term R&D programs.
- Lack of competitiveness in minerals and metals can have negative consequences for the competitiveness of related sectors of U.S. industry, such as electronics and aerospace.

In other industry sectors these arguments have led the U.S. government to develop policies and mechanisms that stimulate government-industry partnerships to advance the development of technology. Such actions have been most prominent in the high-technology and manufacturing fields where technology is the highly visible centerpiece of industrial progress. The minerals and metals industry, on the other hand, has not received this type of attention, despite its obvious importance to the high-technology and manufacturing sectors. The committee believes that there is a legitimate federal role here, as well, and that the same type of government intervention and support being applied in high technology and manufacturing is also warranted to improve the competitiveness of the minerals and metals industry.

MINERALS AND METALS POLICY IN
THE U.S. AND ABROAD

Minerals and Metals Policy in the U.S.

There are many reasons for the federal government to have an interest in the competitiveness of the U.S. minerals and metals industry, including balance of trade, employment, and security of supply. But the federal government has other interests related to the industry, many of which have been expressed as statutory responsibilities. These statutory responsibilities include the following:

• *Land use*—in particular the use of federal lands on which many of the nation's ore reserves are found. Competing uses of those lands, the goals of land management, and questions of fairness in the allocation of land use are all considerations.

• *Environmental protection*—as embodied in various laws regarding clean air and water and resource conservation and recovery. Competing public interests frequently collide in this arena.

• *Public health and safety*—especially in the context of occupational hazards and medical risks encountered in the workplace. Mining is an inherently hazardous industrial activity, and chemical processing (which includes metals extraction and processing) is not far behind in safety risks.

• *National security*—in terms of assured supply of raw materials, independent of the vagaries of politics and economics associated with imports. Especially important here are minerals and metals used in military and civilian applications essential to the national defense that are unavailable or in short supply in domestic reserves.

• *Economic well-being*—in terms of the health and vitality of the U.S. minerals and metals industry.

Because the numerous national policies affecting the minerals and metals industry are not administered by a single agency, there has been no consistent policy governing minerals R&D or supply issues and no effective coordination of many federal activities that affect the industry.

The development of a national minerals and materials policy has been a recurring issue for almost 40 years. In early 1951, when the buildup for the Korean War was hampered by shortages in metals critical to the production of war materiel, President Truman created the President's Commission on Materials Policy (named the Paley Commission after its chairman, William S. Paley). Since then the debate over minerals and materials issues has been kept alive by two commissions; several panels of the National Academy of Sciences (NAS); reports by the Congressional Research Service (CRS), the General Accounting Office, and the Office of Technology Assessment (OTA); and numerous congressional hearings (see Table 5-1). In general, the focus of this attention has been on the supply of raw materials for national security and on the availability of materials needed by domestic manufacturing industries. For the most part the recommendations of the commissions, panels, and agencies have either been ignored from the outset or, when enacted in the form of legislation, the laws have seldom been implemented or enforced.

Three major themes emerge from the four decades of debate over minerals and materials policy. First, U.S. actions should be based on an international free market in materials. In every study, when the policies of interdependence and self-sufficiency are compared, the recommendation has been to accept interdependence. However, there has always been a recognition that the market cannot be depended on for all situations, which leads to the second area of consensus—the development of a materials stockpile to be used when shortages threaten the national security. The third theme of materials policy that has arisen in every study is the need for a national minerals and materials policy organization. Since the Paley Commission, there has been a general consensus that a standing governmental body, capable of cutting across agency boundaries and responsibilities, is needed to coordinate and guide research, regulation, management, and other activities related to the production, use, recovery, and disposal of minerals and materials. With a few brief exceptions, however, efforts to bring minerals and materials policy under one agency have been ignored or opposed by the Executive Branch.

The principal congressional mandate for federally coordinated R&D policy in this area is the Mining and Minerals Policy Act of 1970 (P.L. 91-631), the Surface Mining Act of 1977 (P.L. 95-87) and the State Mining and Minerals

TABLE 5-1 Major Examinations of U.S. Minerals and Metals Policy, 1951–Present

Commissions
  President's Commission on Materials Policy (1951–1952)
  National Commission on Materials Policy (1970–1973)
  National Commission on Supplies and Shortages (1974–1976)
NAS Reports
  National Minerals Policy (NAS, 1975)
  Man, Materials, and the Environment (NAS, 1973)
  Mineral Resources and the Environment (NAS, 1975)
  Materials Science and Engineering for the 1990s: Maintaining Competitiveness
    in the Age of Materials (NAS, 1989)
Congressional Studies and Reports
  Industrial Materials: Technological Problems and Issues for Congress (CRS,
    1972)
  Federal Materials Research and Development: Modernization Institutions and
    Management (CRS, 1975)
  Strategic Materials: Technologies to Reduce U.S. Import Dependence (OTA,
    1985)

Resources Research Institute Program Act of 1984 (P.L. 98-409). The 1984 legislation continued the Mining and Mineral Resources Research Institute (Mineral Institutes) program (Chapter 4) and amended the original act by establishing a mechanism for the coordination of federal, state, and private R&D in minerals and metals. In particular, it established a Committee on Mining and Mineral Research that is to report to the Secretary of the Interior on matters covered by the act. The committee's principal responsibility is to develop and revise a national plan for research in mining and minerals, a plan that assesses federal research in the context of private and academic research and recommends research policies for the Secretary of the Interior.

Although the Committee on Mining and Mineral Research should be a key element in a national minerals and materials policy, its work has had little visibility or impact. This results in part from the fact that the committee is exempted from relevant sections of the Public Advisory Committee Act. Insufficient public oversight and participation in the work of the committee limits the range of perspectives on U.S. minerals and materials research policy. It also subverts the effort to build a public consensus in support of a plan of research that coordinates private, academic, and federal research. (The provisions of the act are summarized in Table 5-2 and described below.)

TABLE 5-2 Major Provisions of the State Mining and Mineral Resources Research Institute Program Act of 1984

Sec. 1221:   Authorization of state allotments to institutes
Sets forth the amount, type, and purpose of grants to states for the establishment of Mineral Institutes.

Sec. 1222:   Research funds to institutes
Authorizes the appropriations and describes the procedures for preparing, reviewing, and selecting research applications (proposals).

Sec. 1223:   Funding Criteria
Describes criteria for continued funding.

Sec. 1224:   Duties of Secretary
Sets forth requirements for the Secretary of Interior to:
   • Prescribe rules and regulations necessary to carry out the provisions of the law; coordinate research by the institutes; indicate important lines of research; and facilitate cooperation among the institutes and between them and other agencies and research centers.
   • Ascertain annually whether funding requirements have been met.
   • Report to Congress annually on the program.

Sec. 1225:   Effect on colleges and universities
Gives assurance that the act will not alter the relationship between host institutions and their state government.

Sec. 1226:   Research
Provides for the following:

• Requires the Secretary to obtain advice and cooperation from other federal, state, and private organizations to ensure that the research conducted under the program is not redundant and to make information on the research freely available.

• Gives assurance that the Secretary is not given authority over programs of other federal agencies.

• Assures that all results of the research are made available to the public and authorizes appropriations for publication.

Sec. 1227:   Center for cataloging
Requires the Secretary to establish a center for cataloging current and projected research in all fields of mining and mineral resources, by federal and nonfederal agencies and to maintain a catalog of such research for public use.

Sec. 1228:   Interagency cooperation
Directs the President to clarify agency responsibilities for mining and mineral resources research and provide for continuing interagency coordination of the research, including identification of technical and manpower needs.

Sec. 1229:   Committee on Mining and Mineral Resources Research
Describes and establishes this committee, making various specific provisions, including:

• Composition of the committee, which the Secretary must appoint.

• A requirement for the committee to consult with the Secretary, and vice versa, on all matters under its purview.

• A requirement that the committee members be compensated for their time and reimbursed for travel expenses.

• A provision that the committee be chaired jointly by the appropriate Assistant Secretary of the Interior and one other committee member.

• A requirement that the committee develop a "national plan for research" in mining and mineral resources and develop and recommend a program to implement the plan, updating the plan annually.

• A stipulation that Section 10 of the Federal Advisory Committee Act (open meetings) does not apply to the committee.

Sec. 1230:   Eligibility criteria
Sets forth criteria that the committee must use regarding eligibility to participate as a Mineral Institute, including:

• The presence of a substantial program of graduate education and research in mining and minerals extraction or closely related fields.

• Evidence of institutional commitment to the program.

• Evidence that the institution can obtain significant industrial funding.

• The presence of an engineering program in mining and minerals extraction that is accredited by the Accreditation Board for Engineering and Technology (or the equivalent).

SOURCE: P.L. 98-409.

Minerals and Metals Policies of Other Countries

Developed Countries

Japan is an industrialized nation with limited domestic mineral resources whose government exerts considerable influence over domestic mining while aggressively seeking to expand its access to external sources of minerals. The government has exclusive power to grant domestic mining rights and leases, which are generally limited to Japanese citizens or corporations (a special treaty is required to grant such rights or leases to a foreign corporation). The granting of mining rights and leases is administered by the Ministry of International Trade and Industry (MITI), which also enforces mine safety and environmental laws. The Japanese government's mineral policy has four aims:

- to secure stable sources of minerals,
- to develop domestic mineral resources systematically,
- to promote development of overseas mineral resources through economic cooperation with mineral-rich developing countries, and
- to stockpile (for economic purposes) minerals that are in short supply.

The Metal Mining Agency of Japan (MMAJ) works closely with the appropriate departments and divisions under MITI to implement these policies. To develop domestic mineral resources, for example, MMAJ conducts geological surveys, while the government subsidizes the costs of private sector exploration. To develop overseas mineral resources, MMAJ operates a Mineral Resources Information Center, conducts surveys of geological structures, finances overseas exploration by private Japanese companies, and cooperates with developing countries on basic surveys of mineral resources. MMAJ also finances and administers the stockpiling program.

Canada ranks first in the world in mine production of nickel and zinc and is the leading source of U.S. imports for 15 significant nonfuel minerals. Most Canadian mineral production (both crude and processed) is for export, accounting for approximately 30 percent of Canada's total exports. As a result, the minerals sector has high visibility and importance in Canadian government policy deliberations. Three broad categories of mineral policy objectives have been established:

- promoting the economic growth and development of the Canadian nonfuel minerals sector by encouraging both the rapid development of mineral resources and the development of mineral processing to increase Canada's share of value-added products;
- developing a minerals policy that would encourage sovereignty and unity (greater Canadian ownership and control and greater contribution of minerals to regional and national development); and

• incorporating concerns about the quality of life and the environment into Canadian minerals policies.

R&D is promoted through tax policy, cost sharing, and direct-grants programs. There are several government research organizations, such as the Canadian Center for Mineral and Energy Technology (CANMET), which is a research and pilot-plant complex that provides mechanisms for government-industry-university collaborative R&D. Foreign-controlled corporations are required to conduct R&D so as to improve Canada's technology base. The Canadian federal government also collects and disseminates minerals information and develops minerals policy through its Ministry of Energy, Mines, and Resources.

Environmental regulations and standards in Canada are similar to those of the United States in both content and strictness. This significantly increases the cost of production, but investment in environmental equipment is frequently subsidized by federal and provincial authorities. Finally, federal-provincial relations are a significant element of Canadian policies toward the minerals sector: provincial governments have their own policy priorities and employ their own policy instruments; these are coordinated by the federal government, but the actions of the provincial governments are more significant in Canadian minerals and metals policy than are state actions in the United States.

Developing Countries

The minerals policies of developing nations differ from those of industrialized nations. The policies of industrialized nations generally relate to extracting lower-grade mineral resources efficiently while protecting the environment. Policy mechanisms most frequently employed include laws encouraging prospecting by the private sector, government surveying for deposits, incentives for investment in development of new sites and in mining equipment, environmental protection, and financing of R&D (either directly or through various forms of subsidy and tax relief). The latter can include planning, coordinating, and information dissemination relating to R&D, whether performed by government itself or by the private sector with government encouragement and financial support.

Technology is seldom the basis for competitiveness in a developing country's minerals and metals industry. As a result, the minerals policies of developing nations are not R&D related. With their typically richer deposits, their policies promote maximizing output and government revenues from the sale of resources. The goals of these policies may include generation of foreign exchange, full employment, development of industrial infrastructure, and use of domestically produced materials and products. Mechanisms for these policies encompass such things as limitations on foreign investment, high extraction taxes, allocation of foreign exchange, and forced employment generation.

ROLE OF THE BUREAU OF MINES

From its inception in 1910, the Bureau of Mines (BOM) has been the principal agency of the federal government for improving productivity and safety in the mining and metals industry. Until the early 1950s each succeeding administration turned to the Bureau for advice on matters of safety and national security. With the proliferation of specialized federal agencies, however, the broad influence of the Bureau began to fade. It has continued to focus on its primary mission of improving mining technology and safety—areas in which the Bureau has been responsible for many important advances (see Table 5-3). But while BOM continues to make technological advances, its recent contributions have been narrower in scope and smaller in impact, and in the past decade there have been fewer of them.

The BOM collects and disseminates statistical data and other information on minerals and metals. It also provides analyses to assist policy makers with decisions regarding land use regulations, environmental policies, and policies that tend to affect the competitiveness of the domestic industry.

TABLE 5-3 Major Technological Contributions by the Bureau of Mines

1948:	Major early contributions to uranium processing
	First commercial production of titanium
1951:	First commercial production of zirconium (used in reactors of nuclear submarines)
1954:	Development of the solvent extraction and electrowinning processes
1950s:	Mine roof bolting
1961:	Development of the ion exchange system for metals recovery
1963:	Flotation treatment of iron ores by selective flocculation
1969:	Heap leaching techniques for low-grade gold ores
1974:	Economical recovery of iron ore from nonmagnetic taconite
1970s:	Vacuum melting and casting process for "space age" metals
	More complete extraction technologies in underground coal
	Coal mine illumination
	Methane drainage
	Self-contained self-rescuers
1980s:	Respirable dust control

Status of the Bureau of Mines

Within the Federal Establishment

The Bureau of Mines has a broad mandate covering not only technology for improved productivity but also land use, environmental protection, health and safety statistical information, policy analysis, and national security. That broad scope occasionally brings a degree of overlap with other federal agencies, taking the form of cooperation as well as contention over responsibility and authority. Examples include the following:

• *Exploration*—The Bureau's research in areas such as ore body definition and characterization is closely related to the U.S. Geological Survey's responsibilities in mineral resource exploration.

• *Health and safety*—The Bureau's research focuses mostly on equipment safety, mining methods, and monitoring; to a degree it coincides with the interests of both the Mine Safety and Health Administration and the National Institute for Occupational Safety and Health.

• *Environmental technology*—The Bureau's interests in surface mining methods, waste prevention and control, and solution mining overlap with those of the Office of Surface Mining Reclamation and Enforcement, the Environmental Protection Agency (EPA), and the Bureau of Land Management.

A basic problem in dealing with competition over agency responsibilities is the Bureau's location within the Department of the Interior, which has a traditional mandate to preserve and maintain public lands. Because the Bureau's mission involves mining, which disturbs and exploits the land, its mission is somewhat at odds with other interests and concerns of the department. This situation apparently results in a lack of strong support for the Bureau in executive branch decisions and congressional hearings.

The changing status of the Bureau within the federal government is reflected by its budget over the past decade (see Figure 5-1). The 1989 appropriation is about 11 percent higher than the 1980 figure in current dollars, but this translates into a full-time equivalent staff level reduction of 20 percent, to 2,348 in 1989 versus 2,942 in 1980. The Bureau's budget has recovered somewhat since 1986, a reflection of increasing congressional support and more effective representation of the Bureau's interests by current Bureau management. Nevertheless, its budget in inflation-adjusted dollars is still far below the level of 1980.

Relationships with Industry

The Bureau of Mines has always been oriented toward the needs of the mining industry, but its preferred role has been to develop technology inter-

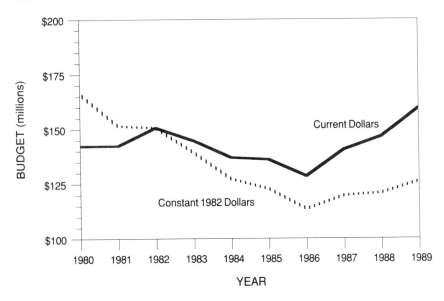

FIGURE 5-1 Budget trends of the Bureau of Mines. Source: Bureau of Mines.

nally and then to transfer it to industry. Only about 5 percent of research at BOM's Mining and Metallurgy Laboratories is contracted out, some of it with industry groups. Recently, the American Mining Congress (AMC) has begun providing BOM with industry input for its in-house programs, and the Mining and Metallurgical Society of America (MMSA) has advised on metallurgical research in Bureau laboratories.

Each BOM laboratory can also point to numerous technologies that it has developed and transferred to industry (see Table 5-4), but the quality and significance of these developments have varied. Specific mechanisms for accomplishing technology transfer to industry include cost-sharing research agreements, special publications, films, seminars, and workshops. In-mine experiments are also cited as an effective device for discussion and technology transfer, although these appear to be few in number. Bureau researchers note a trend toward more frequent publication of their research results in journals with wide public distribution.

Given its legislative mandate, history, and technical capability, the Bureau of Mines is the only source of technological assistance from the federal government by which the U.S. minerals and metals industry can improve its productivity and safety. However, the connection between the Bureau and its industry constituency appears to be weaker than in most other industries. A major problem is a seeming lack of interest and support on the part of industry. Compounding this barrier is the decline of the industrial R&D

infrastructure, which has become so weak that there is often no one to transfer technologies to. The industry as a whole is resistant to introducing new technologies, especially those that are capital intensive and in whose development industry played no role. One of the most effective ways around this dilemma is joint or collaborative research between the Bureau and an individual company or group of companies, a topic that is discussed below.

TABLE 5-4 Bureau of Mines Twin Cities Research Center Technology Transfer Activities

Content	Medium
Discriminating backup alarms	Film
Ground vibration/blasting guidelines	Information circular
Mine subsidence prediction	Workshop
In situ technology	Demonstration
Diesel emission controls	Cooperative agreement
Fire protection systems	Insurance premiums
Blasting safety/effectiveness	Technology transfer seminar
Abrasive water jet technology	License
Enhanced drilling	Outside publication

SOURCE: Twin Cities Research Center, briefing to the committee.

Alternative Institutional Models

The U.S. Geological Survey (USGS) is also organized under the Department of the Interior, but it maintains a considerably greater degree of autonomy than BOM. This is due in part to the nature of its operations, which require offices and field representatives scattered across the United States and in other countries, making it less susceptible to central management. It is also due to its emphasis on the scientific aspects of the minerals industry. The USGS is perceived as an organization of scientists serving in the public interest—the services it performs are easily understood and widely used by companies, farmers, developers, and individuals. This contributes to the perception that the work of the USGS is politically and philosophically neutral, unlike the Bureau of Mines, which has a distinct focus on the needs of the mining industry.

The USGS also conducts many of its operations in collaboration with other government agencies. For example, it is heavily involved in defense mapping work with the Department of Defense (DOD) and in climate and marine geology surveys with the National Oceanic and Atmospheric Administration (NOAA). The USGS performs surveys of energy resources for the Department of Energy (DOE), and surveys mineral resources in conjunction with the BOM, Forest Service, National Parks Service, Fish and Wildlife Service, and Bureau of Indian Affairs. These activities provide both external funding and a partnership with diverse national interests and agencies. This gives the USGS a degree of independence from the specific interests of the Department of the Interior and leads to much greater status and influence with other parts of the federal government.

There are lessons here that might be applicable to BOM. The overlap of interests between the BOM and the USGS, DOD, EPA, DOE, National Aeronautics and Space Administration (NASA), and National Science Foundation (NSF) should suggest ways to initiate long-term joint R&D efforts that require the expertise of both participating agencies. For example, DOE is collaborating with the aluminum industry (which is a major consumer of electricity) in the development of energy-saving aluminum-reduction pilot plants. One can readily envision BOM involved in R&D on the associated process technology.

Another potential model for BOM is the National Institute of Standards and Technology (NIST), which as the National Bureau of Standards earned the respect and confidence of industry through its role in testing new materials and setting technical standards. Like BOM, NIST conducts most of its research in-house and, like the Bureau, is organized as a component of a cabinet department (Commerce) that has diverse interests and responsibilities. Effective interaction with industry has always been a high priority for NIST, which now focuses more strongly than ever on improving the competitiveness of U.S. industry through technology transfer from universities and government laboratories. Under the terms of the Omnibus Trade and Competitiveness Act of 1988, NIST is authorized to create a network of regional affiliates called Manufacturing Technology Centers (MTCs) dedicated to transferring NIST- and university-developed technology (especially in manufacturing) to local and regional businesses. Three MTCs are in place, with as many as 12 envisioned in the authorizing legislation.

NIST has a long history of collaboration with industry through the Industrial Research Associates program. Under this program a private firm may approach NIST with a proposal to carry out joint research with NIST research staff, using NIST facilities, in an area of interest to NIST. In recent years many of the projects have focused on manufacturing technology. Typically, a company sends its researchers to NIST for the duration of the project, although at present some projects are implemented via a data link between the participants. There are currently about 200 projects under the Industrial Research Associates program, each established under a memorandum of understanding. Beyond these programs, the influence of NIST traditionally extends to many technical standards committees organized under various technical and professional societies. Through this mechanism, and those described above, the agency is able to perform a valuable and highly visible service to industry and thereby maintain the respect and cooperation of the industrial community.

Other nations also provide relevant models for the operation of a government agency in the interest of the domestic mining and metals processing industries. One example is the Commonwealth Scientific and Industrial Research Organization (CSIRO) in Australia. Like the Bureau of Mines, CSIRO supports R&D on mining and minerals technology. While there is a central laboratory, regional research stations around the country are the focal point for research activities. CSIRO researchers often work collaboratively with Australian mining and metals companies in on-site testing and analysis operations in company plants. CSIRO staff also work directly with university researchers and with the Australian Minerals Industries Research Association (AMIRA), an industry group, on a variety of research projects.

OPPORTUNITIES FOR ACTION

The pervading message of this report has been that there is a need to improve the technology base of the U.S. minerals and metals industry by increasing the amount and quality of R&D as well as the speed with which results are transferred into industrial applications. The committee has identified five areas for action that it believes can improve the development and implementation of significant technological advances to strengthen the competitiveness of the U.S. minerals and metals industry:

• establish an advisory committee to provide expert advice for the Bureau of Mines;
• promote collaborative R&D, both within the industry and among industry, universities, and government;
• encourage mechanisms for developing consensus within the industry on the directions for basic and applied research;
• stimulate rapid technology transfer; and
• improve the planning and coordination process within the Bureau of Mines.

Expert Advice to the Bureau of Mines

The Bureau of Mines interacts with other organizations as necessary to carry out its assigned functions and projects, but it has found it difficult to promote substantive debate about the future of mining and minerals policy. The only public body with a potential advisory role is the Committee on Mining and Mineral Resources Research, but to date it has not used the authority of its legislative mandate to fulfill this role. The committee is chaired jointly by the Assistant Secretary of the Interior for Water and Science and one other committee member; the membership includes representatives of the BOM, the USGS, the National Academies of Sciences and Engineering (NAS/NAE), the NSF, at least two university representatives, at least two representatives of the mining industry, one working miner, and one representative of the conservation community. Public representation has been even further restricted in practice by the appointment of former government officials to the committee: two former directors of the BOM currently sit on the committee, one representing industry and the other academe. This structure limits the committee's ability to contribute outside ideas and advice to the Bureau and its research programs.

The effectiveness of the committee also depends on the resources provided to it by the Department of the Interior. Since the administration has been recommending the elimination of the Mineral Institutes program for several years, no provision has been made for funding the work of the committee; funding by Congress has focused strictly on the institutes themselves. The committee has no staff, nor has it made significant use of advice from experts and expert groups in industry and academe. The committee's work realistically requires funds to compensate its members for their time and expenses.

These considerations all point to the need for the Department of the Interior to establish a new standing advisory committee reporting directly to the director of the Bureau of Mines. This committee should advise the director not only on the content and direction of research but also on any other Bureau programs and policy matters. The committee should consist of interested and knowledgeable senior individuals entirely from outside the federal government—with a particular emphasis on industry. Once again, if this committee is to carry out its responsibilities effectively, funds must be provided for its maintenance. The committee must have staff support, and it must be able to invite contributions from nongovernmental experts.

Promoting Collaborative Research and Development

Collaborative (or cooperative or shared) R&D, whether between government and industry, or among industrial firms, or involving government, universities, and industry, is not a new idea. The first formal industrial collaborative R&D effort was established in England around 1775 by Josiah Wedgewood, the famous potter, in order to seek better glazes and glazing techniques. Today the concept of cooperative research has become fashionable, not only in the United States but in Japan and Europe, especially in the high-technology and manufacturing fields. Some of the best-known consortia are in electronics—the Microelectronics and Computer Technology Corporation, the Semiconductor Research Corporation, and Sematech.

Other consortia exist in automotive materials and polymers, biotechnology, robotics, energy, and other emerging fields. Even so, no more than 3 percent of U.S. R&D funding flows through consortia, with about 85 percent of that amount being spent in regulated oil, gas, and electric industries. Thus, although increasingly prevalent, cooperative research is still not a primary mechanism for R&D in the United States.

The common denominator in all these arrangements is the perceived need to pool resources to develop the fundamental or "precompetitive" knowledge that participating companies can then apply to increase their competitiveness, usually vis-à-vis foreign industries. An underlying theme is that university research often has not connected in the past in a useful way with industry needs. Cooperative R&D forces the participants to consider where they want to be in the future; it ensures a focus on actual industry needs; it facilitates effective transfer of the technologies; and it helps to build a corresponding research capability in the participating companies. But there are also drawbacks: tension can easily develop between the wish to cooperate and the need to compete; it can be difficult to transfer technologies into company laboratories and products; and cost sharing can be problematical when different-sized companies are involved.

To date, the track record of consortia is mixed. Experience has shown that cooperative R&D can be a supplement to in-house R&D but not a substitute. Certainly those companies without an R&D base of their own and a core of technical personnel as receptors will not benefit from consortia. Similarly, for all participants to feel a sense of ownership of the research projects requires people who can act as technology transfer agents between the consortium and the company laboratory. The line between precompetitive research and commercial R&D is vague, which emphasizes the need for care in selecting projects. For this reason cooperative R&D should focus on generic technologies that can benefit all participants about equally.

While U.S. mining companies compete strenuously both in exploration and marketing, the history of mining technology has been one of cooperation rather than competition. Most of the subindustries are distinguished by a remarkably free interchange of ideas and data. Even where patented technology is involved, innovations and improvements are commonly made available on reasonable terms, except for special processes that would impart a distinct competitive advantage to the developer. Mining thus seems to be an excellent candidate for cooperative R&D ventures like the following:

• The American Mining Congress (AMC) has recently taken a lead role in addressing the technology needs of the mining and metals extraction industries. AMC is currently exploring the role that it could play in fostering industry research projects, coordinating industry research programs, and serving as a clearinghouse for information on emerging technologies and technological needs.

• The Mining and Excavation Research Institute (MERI) is a consortium of universities organized under the American Society of Mechanical Engineers. Incorporated in New York as an independent not-for-profit research, education, and service institute, its aim is "to spur development of a variety of systems for intelligent remote-controlled mining and excavation via a university-industry consortium." Formed in 1987, MERI now has 12 university and 4 corporate members. Despite its limited funding and staff resources, MERI shows promise for being the kind of enterprise that the U.S. mining and minerals industry needs.

• The International Copper Research Association (INCRA) was established in 1959 and presently has 25 corporate members. Its 1989 R&D budget was $3 million. Most of the research it sponsors at commercial and university laboratories is on end products and applications, with a view to expanding the products and uses of copper. The INCRA has recently been folded into a new organization, the International Copper Association, which coordinates the market development activities of the various copper trade associations around the world.

• The American Iron and Steel Institute (AISI), founded in 1908, is a trade association, but it also carries out extensive technical work. R&D represents more than half its budget. This R&D is carried out in three main categories: sponsored research at university research centers, such as the Steel Resource Center at Northwestern University (totaling more than $1 million per year); collaborative technology projects (currently totaling about $2 million per year in eight collaborative projects); and the Steel Initiative described earlier, to which AISI will contribute about $10 million or one third of the cost over 3 years.

• The International Lead-Zinc Research Organization (ILZRO) sponsors research designed to expand the markets for lead and zinc by finding new uses of these metals. All research is contracted out. With 36 producer members (mining and smelting companies) as well as 25 end-user members, its research budget was about $4 million in 1989.

Other metals industry associations also sponsor research, including the Aluminum Association, the Nickel Development Institute (in Canada), the Copper Development Association, the Metal Powder Industries Federation, and the International Tin Research Association (in Great Britain). User industries (e.g., automotive and aerospace industries) also do research that generates demand and therefore drives research, mostly in semifabricated parts. Across all of these and other organizations, however, most of the research sponsored by the industry associations is concerned with expanding the market for existing applications and end products. Relatively little of it addresses the need for new technologies to improve productivity and processes (the $30 million Steel Initiative is an exception). In addition, the level of funding for these cooperative activities is too low to support research programs that could have a major impact on the competitiveness of this industry.

Fundamental breakthroughs in technology usually require a broader interdisciplinary approach to R&D. It is difficult for the minerals and metals industry, divided into subindustries and competing firms, to provide long-term guidance for such research. As a result, this is an occasion when it is appropriate for government to take the lead. There are several justifications for federal support of R&D in the mining and metals industry:

• The benefits of successful R&D cannot be fully captured by the firm investing in the research.
• The time horizon of the effort must be longer than companies would be likely to undertake on their own.
• The risk of failure is so high as to deter companies from research that would otherwise be an attractive investment (high-risk, high-reward).
• The work is directed at public interests, such as the environment, that companies have less incentive to pursue on their own or, when pursued, may be perceived as not being objective.

There are no ideal models for government-industry-university cooperation in the mining and metals industry. The Department of Commerce has counted more than 125 consortia established under the National Cooperative Research Act of 1984, representing every conceivable structure and ranging from 2 to 59 members. Experience has shown that multiple bilateral partnerships are easier to manage than a consortium because the interest groups are smaller. Japanese experience appears to reflect this perception; the Japanese government prefers "managed joint research," in which the research is divided among participating companies. The German Fraunhofer Gesellschaft represents a successful model for government-industry collaboration: the states as well as the federal government provide funding; these federally chartered research organizations are disbanded as their usefulness declines.

The decline of industry research laboratories, described in Chapter 4, makes it more difficult for the U.S. government to conduct joint research with industry in the processing area. Other research must be done on the pilot scale, which means that pilot facilities will have to be built at universities or other sites. These cautions do not mean that government-industry collaboration cannot succeed, however. The joint BOM/ASARCO/Freeport project on in situ mining of copper oxide ore (recently joined by the University of Arizona) is a good example of productive collaborative R&D. Likewise, the steel initiative operated through the DOE is an excellent example of government-sponsored research involving various forms of government-industry, government-university, and intragovernmental cooperation (DOE and NIST).

The national laboratories represent a major potential resource, especially for some aspects of materials research, and their sponsoring agencies (mostly DOE) have been urging U.S. industry to pursue collaborative research with them. However, industry has shown relatively little interest, and thus far the laboratories seem to have been trying harder to link up with industry than the reverse. More directly relevant is the potential for industry to work collaboratively with the Bureau-supported Mineral Institutes, especially those that are configured into GMTCs. As noted in Chapter 4, industry involvement in these centers has been surprisingly light; for example, industrial funding of the GMTC for pyrometallurgy has totaled only $66,400 since its establishment in 1982. This amount, although small, is about average for the centers.

The Bureau's own Mining and Metallurgy Laboratories have also done some collaborative work with industry. For example, the Twin Cities Research Center recently collaborated with industry on the in situ leaching demonstration project mentioned above. The Pittsburgh Research Center is well known for its collaborative work with industry in mine design and excavation techniques, using the laboratory's fully instrumented test mine. However, these examples are the exception rather than the rule. Before they would be attractive to industry in general as partners in research, the Mining and Metallurgy Laboratories would need to update their R&D portfolio and bring in younger researchers as well as more staff from industry. The formula for success at DOE laboratories has often been for the laboratory staff to begin a line of research at the fundamental level and then to bring in the industry researchers as the work becomes progressively more developmental—what has been termed a phase-in, phase-out approach. It would probably be beneficial for the BOM laboratories to communicate closely with the DOE laboratories on problems of mutual interest, both for the sake of the research and for the opportunity to observe new ways of working with industry.

Developing Consensus Within the
Minerals and Metals Policy Community

The mining and metals industry has no constituency sufficiently well organized to press effectively for its own interests and those of the nation. This is one reason for the failure of previous policy studies to achieve their intended results. In the 1970s a network of key individuals in public and private institutions maintained a sense of community in the area of mining and minerals policy, including R&D policy. Over time, however, transfers and retirements reduced the effectiveness of the network, and a shift of attention from minerals and metals to a broader interest in advanced materials has further dispersed the traditional minerals community. At present there are special-interest communities within the mining industry and the academic environment, but there is no larger community that shares a common interest in an effective national mining and minerals policy. Rather, the various special-interest groups pursue their own agendas for research, import restrictions, etc. It is not that these groups lack broader concerns but rather that no single group is able to provide the forum and agenda for discussion of those concerns.

Without a broadly based consensus about the importance of a national mining and minerals policy, support for mining and minerals R&D will remain fragmented and ineffective. A successful model for consensus building in mining and minerals policy is the ongoing series of materials policy conferences sponsored by the Federation of Materials Societies held in Henniker, New Hampshire, and more recently in Fredericksburg, Virginia. Another example is the biennial conference sponsored by the USGS on issues related to the exclusive economic zone. In both cases the sponsoring agencies provide a forum for the gathering of a wide community that shares a common interest in development of an effective national policy. Without some such forum it is unlikely that a broadly supported mining and minerals policy can be developed.

Stimulating Rapid Technology Transfer

Companies have no incentive to participate in R&D consortia if they cannot realize a tangible return on their investment. Such benefits depend significantly on a company's ability to incorporate the advances made through research into their own use of technology. The process of technology transfer, and the success with which it is achieved, is therefore critical to the value of collaborative R&D as perceived by industry. It has been widely noted, however, that the United States excels at generating fundamental knowledge, while other nations (especially Japan) excel at putting that knowledge to practical use. Thus, improving the speed and efficiency of technology transfer into U.S. firms is vital to their competitiveness, in the minerals and metals industry as well as in other more technology-intensive industries.

Close involvement by industry in the technology development process is the surest way to make certain that U.S. industry has a head start in the application of new knowledge. Collaborative research, at least when it involves a small number of participants, is valuable for providing this inside track. However, with a larger number of participants the lack of company control over the results of research is a drawback, since it is then proportionately harder to restrict access to important findings. For this same reason the participation of foreign firms or those with mixed ownership, including U.S.-based multinationals, is also a difficult issue.

One mechanism to stimulate technology transfer would be targeted research. Certain kinds of technology offer an inherently greater relative advantage to U.S. industry than to foreign industry (see Chapter 3). For example, environmental regulations are more stringent in the United States than in most other countries; consequently, research on environmental systems, processes, and control technologies is potentially more beneficial to U.S. companies. Because of high insurance and litigation costs, research to enhance worker health and safety also benefits U.S. producers disproportionately. A similar rationale holds for research on automation and computer control, which address high labor costs, and processes relevant to low-grade ores.

Another mechanism for stimulating more rapid and effective technology transfer would be the availability of more timely and comprehensive information about ongoing research and technological advances in mining and minerals technology around the world, as several trade groups (e.g., the Copper Development Association) do in limited ways now. Such a mechanism was called for by the 1984 act: "The Secretary shall establish a center for cataloguing current and projected scientific research in all fields of mining and mineral resources" (P.L. 98-409, paragraph 7). The Bureau of Mines already collects such information in an informal way, and it is currently working on faster dissemination under the proposed information upgrade in the Information and Analysis Directorate. The American Mining Congress also hopes to establish itself as a clearinghouse of information on R&D. However, none of these plans has come to fruition yet. What is needed is a computerized data base, accessible by telephone, containing information on recent and current research worldwide, industry production and demand statistics, demand trend analyses, technology assessments, and other types of statistical and analytical information.

Improved Planning and Coordination

Over past decades the Bureau of Mines established a strong record as a center of excellence and innovation. However, in recent years it has become increasingly limited in its role in the minerals and metals community, and this has caused problems with both the substance and effectiveness of its research. Two problems appear to be central: a lack of planning and a lack of coordination among various groups.

The development of a national plan for mining and minerals R&D is one of the legislated responsibilities of the Committee o Mining and Mineral Resources Research. However, the existing national plan, put forward by the committee in its first annual report, and updated in successive annual reports, is not a true plan. It is merely a program mission statement with accompanying general recommendations regarding the need for interagency coordination and continued federal funding.

The plan envisioned under the authorizing legislation is intended to identify and recommend activities for BOM that fit into the broader picture of industry and academic research. To carry out this planning function, however, there must be communication from industry and academe about the needs of the industry and the capabilities and limitations of the industry and academic research establishments to fulfill those needs. There must also be adequate coordination of roles and research programs across and among those sectors.

Cutbacks in long-term industry R&D have left industry needs for technology ill defined. If BOM, or state agencies and academic institutions for that matter, is to contribute to the technology base for the future domestic mining industry, there must be effective collaboration on the identification of research needs. Regardless of the skills and experience of BOM personnel, the development of a long-term research agenda for the mining industry must be a collaborative exercise involving the potential consumers of R&D as well as other researchers. Such collaboration should extend to other interested federal agencies, such as the Departments of Agriculture, Interior (USGS and BOM), Commerce, Energy, and Defense; EPA; and NSF.

At present this vital communication and collaboration is not taking place. BOM is not consulted on matters in which it has expertise, nor does it appear to contribute to the planning or decisions of other agencies. Examples abound: there was only minimal interaction between the International Trade Agency and BOM during negotiations on U.S.-Canada tariffs that affect the minerals industry; EPA made little use of BOM's expertise when it was developing regulations to deal with mine wastes. The expenditure by Congress from the Stockpile Transaction Fund for university research in strategic and critical materials, with no attempt at linkage with Bureau programs, is a clear instance of the lack of coordination that now prevails.

In the past the Committee on Materials (COMAT), operating under the Office of Science and Technology Policy, has attempted to achieve interagency coordination. However, COMAT has tended to focus on advanced materials rather than minerals and commodity metals. The Bureau of Mines is the logical focal point of federal interest in mining- and metals-related R&D and as such should be the lead actor in interagency planning and coordination. The 1984 act provides a mandate for interagency cooperation and implies a mandate for the Secretary of the Interior to take the lead role (P.L. 98-409, paragraphs 6 and 8).

At the same time, however, BOM must recognize that influence and coordination are two-way streets. On the one hand, the Bureau needs to aggressively seek out a new role for itself as a source of information and advice on all matters involving the minerals and metals industry. To do so, however, it will have to develop its own clearinghouse of comprehensive and accessible information as described above. It must also insist on its place in the making of legislation and in the planning and implementation of federal programs that affect the industry.

On the other hand, the Bureau must open itself up to, in fact actively seek out, external information and advice in making its own policies and decisions. In this sense the establishment of the advisory committee (recommendation 9 in Chapter 6) could be the model for a broader openness on the part of BOM. By encouraging wider involvement in the planning, coordination, and conduct of research, the Secretary of the Interior and BOM can promote consensus among a larger body of producers and researchers about the value of the proposed research. This in turn would result in greater support for the program and BOM—both political and financial—from federal and state governments and from industry.

6

Recommendations

The committee's recommendations address the roles of industry, academe, and government in a coherent and synergistic national program of mining and minerals research and development.

INDUSTRY AND ACADEME

1. Industry Support for Collaborative Research and Development

Mechanisms for conducting cooperative research and development (R&D) are the most promising and practical way to reestablish the flow of technology into the U.S. minerals and metals industry. The committee recommends that the industry consider the formation of consortia to pursue research that is too complex, high risk, and/or expensive for individual companies to pursue alone. Industry collaborative research should focus on broadly defined generic problems offering potentially equal benefits to all participants (e.g., comminution, flotation, and pollution mitigation). Universities and other research organizations that are able to contribute productively should also participate as partners in this research. The Bureau of Mines could play a key role as coordinator, as research participant, or as clearinghouse for information on research needs and directions.

2. Industry Involvement with Academic Research Programs

Industry should seek ways to benefit from the research capabilities of the university-based Generic Mineral Technology Centers (GMTCs). Company representatives should visit the centers, for example, and industry and trade associations should brief GMTC personnel on the technology needs of the industry. Further productive interactions could include personnel exchanges, grant funding, grants (or sharing) of equipment, collaborative and/or contracted research, and consulting. Industry should also support the development and application of promising technological advances by the GMTCs, the Mineral Institutes, and the Mining Advanced Research Initiative (see below) through joint ventures and loans of equipment, materials, and personnel to support prototype testing. Locating a substantial research facility such as a pilot-scale plant at a university (e.g., at one of the GMTCs) would catalyze this type of interaction. Professional societies could promote industry-university collaboration by sponsoring panels with industry and university participants on topics of potential joint benefit.

3. Stability of University Programs

Universities must strive to maintain distinct programs of research and education in minerals- and metals-related disciplines, even during downturns in the business cycle of the industry. To do this researchers will have to take full advantage of every available source of funding and support from government and industry, including new as well as traditional sources. This may involve, for example, redesigning research projects from the specific to the general (e.g., broadening research on mining techniques to encompass tunneling and excavation processes that are applicable to a broad range of problems) in order to fit the research interests of agencies such as the National Science Foundation (NSF) and the Department of Energy (DOE). To maintain an influx of high-quality students, universities must also find creative ways to change the image of the mining and metals field in the view of prospective students. Cooperation with industry is one of the key factors here.

4. Interuniversity Coordination and Collaboration in Research

University research programs in this field are small, and there is little support, financially or economically, for interuniversity coordination or collaboration. Professional societies should take an active role in bringing academic researchers together to discuss current research programs and needs and to build a sense of community within the field. These efforts could be conducted in cooperation with the Minerals and Metals Community Forum (see below).

BUREAU OF MINES AND OTHER AGENCIES

5. Advanced Research Initiative for Mining and Minerals

To provide the domestic industry with opportunities for an effective technology-based competitiveness strategy, the Bureau of Mines should sponsor a program of R&D directed solely at basic and exploratory research on "breakthrough" technologies, not only to improve productivity but also to contribute to mine safety, health, and environmental protection. This new activity should be funded at a level representing a substantial fraction, perhaps 10 to 15 percent of the Bureau's R&D budget. Its staff should be small and innovative; research selection and evaluation should be under Bureau control. The system for reviewing proposals and research should include specialists from a broader range of disciplines than is customary for agencies that fund basic research. The research agenda should combine in-house research with university, corporate, and collaborative research programs.

Ideally, this component of the Bureau's research would be programmatically distinct from existing Bureau research programs and should have high priority within the Bureau. Although it could be organized as an office under the research directorate, the program director should report to the director of the Bureau of Mines. New concepts should be pursued that have the potential to revolutionize the entire process from mining to metals extraction. The Bureau's advisory committee (see below) should be consulted in the selection of research initiatives, which should include long-range research on high-risk, high-payoff topics where success is not guaranteed. The program should recognize the potential value of pilot-scale facilities to prove concepts while strengthening both the technology base in industry and industry's ability to receive and implement new technologies.

6. Maintaining Relevance of Research by Mineral Institutes and GMTCs to National Needs

The Bureau should take a more active role in the Mineral Institutes program by providing leadership in identifying the national research needs of the minerals and metals industry. Such leadership would include promoting the participation of industry associations and academe in identifying these needs. The objectives of this effort should be (1) to achieve a consensus on long-term research goals that would be likely to yield significant returns on the nation's investment in minerals-related research and (2) to focus the attention and efforts of the network of Mineral Institutes and GMTCs on topics that may contribute to the long-term needs of a competitive domestic mining and minerals industry. In order to exert this leadership role the administration should include funding of the Mineral Institutes program in the budget request for the Department of the Interior.

7. Funding of University Research

It is essential to maintain the university research base supporting technological advances in the minerals and metals industry. As the prime federal agency focused on this industry, the Bureau of Mines should continue to channel funds, both budgeted and specially appropriated, to university research centers and institutes, including those institutions not traditionally associated with mining-related programs. All such programs should be funded at reasonably predictable levels for a sufficient length of time to have a chance of succeeding; they should be subject to peer review and should be monitored. Line-item funding benefiting individual institutions should be avoided. One major objective of this funding should be to produce more mining engineers, extractive metallurgists, and geoscientists at all degree levels to meet the nation's future needs for technologically sophisticated technical workers as well as university researchers and educators.

8. Focus of Bureau of Mines Research

A technology-based competitiveness strategy must emphasize knowledge and technologies that will benefit U.S. producers more than their foreign competitors. For example, advanced mining systems can take advantage of the U.S. work force, which is both more highly educated and more expensive than the labor available in developing countries; mining and processing technology can address environmental concerns while reducing the costs of compliance with environmental standards; and exploration and mining technology can be designed to be appropriate to the geological formations of the United States.

Among the research areas of high priority are ore genesis and deposition, in situ mining by hydrometallurgical and biotechnological means, intelligent mining systems, and techniques for more energy-efficient processing. The Bureau should not duplicate work conducted at universities and other government laboratories, but it should ensure that gaps in research are filled by its own research activities, by encouraging academic and industry researchers to focus on appropriate topics, and by collaborative projects with industry. The Bureau should focus on the development of technologies that can be applied by the mining and metals industry and its major subindustries. It should also address the problem of transferring research from the laboratory to the field by facilitating the transfer of technology through its information dissemination programs and through direct contact and collaboration with industry researchers.

9. Advisory Committee

The committee believes that the director of the Bureau of Mines could profit greatly from objective outside advice on the direction and nature of Bureau programs and policies, comparable to the advice received by heads of other federal agencies in technical mission areas. To that end the Bureau should establish an advisory committee consisting of leaders from the mining and metals industry and other industries, universities, and public-interest groups involved in various minerals and metals issues. Representatives of government agencies should be invited as observers but should not serve as members of the committee. The committee should report regularly to the director, advising on the direction and content of Bureau programs, including research, industry problems, relevant advances in technology, information needs, and policy priorities. Staff support and travel funds should be included in the budget of the Bureau of Mines. This advisory committee should be subject to all provisions of the Public Advisory Committee Act. Such a committee would have a broader responsibility than the current Committee on Mining and Minerals Resources Research, which was created by the legislation establishing the Mineral Institutes program and which reports to the Secretary of the Interior, the President, and the Congress.

10. Visiting Committees

Action should also be taken to reestablish the Bureau of Mines as a leading research organization that is respected for the quality of its work and its contribution to national interests in technology, economy, environment, health, and safety. To this end the director of the Bureau should ensure that organizations or groups of individuals will serve as visiting committees to review and evaluate the research programs of the Bureau's in-house Mining and Metallurgy Laboratories in terms of their scientific merit and research operations. These visiting committees should include specialists in research and relevant technical fields, from both academe and industry. The committees should submit their evaluations to the director, who should discuss them with the advisory committee described above.

11. Minerals and Metals Community Forum

The domestic industry would benefit from better communication and a shared view of the technical and policy needs and interests of the various sectors of the minerals and metals community. To this end the Bureau should convene biennially a national minerals and metals forum. Broad participation of industry, academe, government, and local and regional representatives should be encouraged. The forum should seek to establish a sense of community among the participants, identify major technical and policy problems and issues facing the industry over the next 5 years, and disseminate information about research being conducted at the Bureau or under its sponsorship. Professional societies—such as the Society for Mining, Metallurgy and Exploration; the Minerals, Metals and Materials Society; the Federation of Materials Societies; the Mining and Metallurgical Society of America; and similar organizations—should be encouraged to participate in the planning, conduct, and follow-up of the forum. An important goal of this effort should be to engage the active participation of other federal agencies with a stake in the health of the minerals and metals industry, including the Department of Energy, the National Institute of Standards and Technology, the Department of Defense, the Department of Commerce, the National Science Foundation, and the National Aeronautics and Space Administration.

12. Enhanced Technical Information

Another important way in which the Bureau should help to strengthen the competitiveness of the domestic mining and minerals industry is through improved collection, analysis, and dissemination of minerals and metals data including research information worldwide. This may require enhanced capability to translate and evaluate foreign research publications.

Clearinghouse for Government Research. The center for cataloging research in mining and minerals, mandated by P.L. 98-409 in 1984, has not been established. To fill this important need the Bureau should become a clearinghouse for information about minerals-related research conducted or sponsored by all agencies of the U.S. government—including work in progress. It should also establish a process for disseminating information about foreign research programs and technical advances gathered by the Departments of State, Commerce, and Energy; by NSF; and by other government agencies. In the case of evaluation of research in progress, nearly immediate availability is essential.

Current efforts by the Bureau of Mines to utilize electronic information systems to prepare and disseminate minerals data more quickly may serve as a demonstration of new technologies that could be applied to the clearinghouse operation. The "Information Upgrade" proposed by the Bureau for initiation in FY 1991 is highly relevant, as it includes plans for instituting electronic information systems as an alternative to hard-copy publication.

Information Monitoring and Assessment Functions. As part of its technical mission relating to the competitiveness of the minerals and metals industry, the Bureau should further emphasize data collection and dissemination for analysis planning, including

- gathering and evaluating production and demand statistics on these industries, domestic and foreign;
- establishing and maintaining a data base of current demand, which will allow projection of future demand under a range of scenarios;
- publishing timely analyses of trends in demand for minerals and metals;
- monitoring worldwide industry R&D capabilities and advances; and
- assessing new and emerging technologies and making the results available in timely and accessible forms.

Analytical Support for Government Policy-making. As the principal federal repository of information and expertise about the technology and economics of the mining and metals industry, the Bureau should participate in the analysis and debate of government policies such as environmental, land use, or trade policies that affect, or are affected by, the industry. The Secretary of the Interior should actively promote the inclusion of the Bureau in all interagency groups addressing such policies.

Appendix

Biographical Sketches of Committee Members

ALVIN W. TRIVELPIECE is a Vice President of Martin Marietta Systems, Inc., and the Director of Oak Ridge National Laboratory. He received his B.S. from California Polytechnic State College and his M.S. and Ph.D. in Electrical Engineering from California Institute of Technology. During his professional career, Dr. Trivelpiece has been a faculty member at the University of California, Berkeley; Professor of Physics at the University of Maryland, College Park; Vice President of Engineering and Research at Maxwell Laboratories; Corporate Vice President at Scientific Applications, Inc.; Director of the Office of Energy Research, U.S. Department of Energy; and Executive Officer of the American Association for the Advancement of Science.

ROBERT R. BEEBE is senior Vice President of Homestake Mining Company. He received his B.S. and M.S. in Metallurgical Engineering from the Montana School of Mines. Before Homestake, Mr. Beebe was Vice President of Newmont Mining, Vice President of Marcona Corporation, and CEO of Carpco, Inc. Mr. Beebe is a past President of the Mining and Metallurgical Society of America and is a member of the National Academy of Engineering.

GEORGE S. ANSELL is President of the Colorado School of Mines. He received his B.Met.E., M.Met.E., and Ph.D. in Metallurgical Engineering from Rensselaer Polytechnic Institute. Prior to accepting the presidency of Colorado School of Mines, Dr. Ansell was Robert W. Hunt Professor of

131

Metallurgical Engineering, Chairman of the Materials Division, and Dean of Engineering at Rensselaer Polytechnic Institute.

NATHANIEL ARBITER is President of Arbiter Associates, Inc., Consultants, and Adjunct Professor of Metallurgy at the University of Utah. He was previously Director of Research and Chief Metallurgist with Anaconda (1968-1977), Professor of Mineral Engineering (now Emeritus) at Columbia's Krumb School of Mines (1951-1968), and Research Metallurgist for Phelps Dodge (1944-1951) and Battelle Institute (1943-1944). He is a member of the National Academy of Engineering, Honorary Member of American Institute of Metallurgical, Mining and Petroleum Engineers, and a Distinguished Member of the Society of Manufacturing Engineers and has received numerous awards and honors from the latter two organizations.

PATRICK R. ATKINS is Director of Environmental Control and Engineering at ALCOA. He received his B.S. in Civil Engineering from the University of Kentucky, and his M.S. in Sanitary Engineering and Ph.D. in Environmental Engineering from Stanford University. Prior to joining ALCOA, Dr. Atkins was on the faculty of the Environmental Health Engineering Department at the University of Texas, Austin.

R. STEPHEN BERRY is James Franck Distinguished Service Professor at the University of Chicago. He received his A.B., A.M., and Ph.D. in Chemistry from Harvard University. Previously, Dr. Berry was a member of the faculties of Harvard University, University of Michigan, and Yale University. He is a member of the National Academy of Sciences and a MacArthur Fellow.

PETER CANNON is President of Conductus. He received his B.Sc. in Mathematics and Chemistry and Ph.D. in Physical Sciences from the University of London. Previous to his position at Conductus, Dr. Cannon was Vice-President for Research and Chief Scientist at Rockwell International Corporation.

JAMES ECONOMY is Head of the Materials Science and Engineering Department at the University of Illinois at Urbana-Champaign. He received his B.S. from Wayne State University and his Ph.D. in Chemistry from the University of Maryland. Previous to his current position, Dr. Economy was Manager of Polymer Science and Technology at IBM. He is a member of the National Academy of Engineering.

JAMES A. FORD recently retired as Vice President at SELEE to become an independent consultant. He received his B.S., M.S., and Ph.D. in Metallurgical Engineering from the University of Michigan. Dr. Ford was Associate Director of the Metals Research Laboratories at Olin Corporation, Vice President of Research and Development at Conalco, Manager of Research and Development of the Composite Can Division of Boise Cascade Corporation, Director of Technology for the Engineered Products Group of Cabot Corporation, and Director of Technology for Aerojet Ordnance of Tennessee.

NORMAN A. GJOSTEIN is Director of the Powertrain and Materials Research Laboratory at the Ford Motor Company. He received his B.S. and M.S. from the Illinois Institute of Technology and a Ph.D. in Metallurgical Engineering from Carnegie Mellon University. He is a member of the National Academy of Engineering.

BRUCE A. KENNEDY is Managing Director of P. T. Perlsart Management Services in Jakarta, Indonesia. He received his B.Sc. and A.R.S.M. in Mining Engineering from Imperial College, University of London. Previous to Perlsart, Mr. Kennedy was Vice President of Golder Associates and President of ASAMERA Minerals Inc. of Canada.

WILLIAM W. LEWIS is a partner in the management consulting firm of McKinsey and Company. He received his B.S. from Virginia Polytechnic Institute and State University, and was a Rhodes Scholar at Oxford University from which he received a D.Phil. in Theoretical Physics in 1966. His previous experience includes positions as Associate Provost for Resource Planning at Princeton University; Director of the Office of Analytical Studies, University of California, Berkeley; Senior Operations Officer, World Bank; Principal Deputy Assistant Secretary for Program Analysis and Evaluation, U.S. Department of Defense; and Assistant Secretary for Policy and Evaluation, U.S. Department of Energy.

JAMES S. MOOSE is a Senior Industrial Specialist with the World Bank. He received an A.B. and Ph.D. in Economics from Harvard University and an M.A. from Oxford University. Previous to the World Bank, Dr. Moose was Vice President of Loomis Sayles, Deputy Assistant Secretary of the U.S. Department of Energy, and Manager of Strategic Planning at Standard Oil of Ohio.

HAROLD W. PAXTON is the U.S. Steel Professor of Carnegie Mellon University. He received a B.Sc. and an M.Sc. from the University of Manchester and a Ph.D. in Metallurgy from the University of Birmingham. Previously, Dr. Paxton was Vice President of Corporate Research and Technology Assessment at U.S. Steel. He is a member of the National Academy of Engineering.

JOHN E. TILTON is Coulter Professor and Head of the Department of Mineral Economics, Colorado School of Mines. He received his B.A. from Princeton University and M.A. and Ph.D. in Economics from Yale University. Previously, Dr. Tilton was a member of the faculty at the University of Maryland, a Research Associate in the Economic Studies Division of the Brookings Institution, a Staff Analyst in the Manpower Planning and Research Division of the Office of the Secretary of Defense, and a Professor of Mineral Economics at Pennsylvania State University.

ALAN D. ZUNKEL is President of A. D. Zunkel Consultants, Inc. He received a B.S. from the Missouri School of Mines and an M.S. and D.Sc. in Metallurgical Engineering from the Colorado School of Mines. Previously, he was General Superintendent of St. Joe Minerals Company, Manager of Minerals Processing at Exxon Minerals Company, consulting metallurgical engineer for Jan H. Reimer and Associates USA, and Manager of Minerals Business Development for Nerco Minerals Company.

Index